Ace Bourke was born in Sydney in 1946. He has become one of Australia's leading art curators, a pioneer in the field of Aboriginal art and a colonial art specialist, staging numerous critically acclaimed exhibitions. Ace hopes to immerse himself again in wildlife and conservation projects, to help address the world's urgent environmental issues. He lives in Sydney with his two cats.

John Rendall is a sixth-generation Australian, and currently divides his time between London and Sydney. John continues his commitment to the George Adamson Wildlife Preservation Trust and is a member of the Royal Geographical Society in London. He has been involved in travel-focussed public relations, concentrating on conservation projects, lodges and reserves in Africa. John's three children share his passion for wildlife and conservation.

D1056279

www.**rbooks**.co.uk

A Lion Called Christian

Anthony Bourke & John Rendall

BANTAM BOOKS

LONDON • TORONTO • SYDNEY • AUCKLAND • JOHANNESBURG

TRANSWORLD PUBLISHERS
61–63 Uxbridge Road, London W5 5SA
A Random House Group Company
www.rbooks.co.uk

**A LION CALLED CHRISTIAN
A BANTAM BOOK: 9780553820607**

First published in Great Britain
in 1971 by William Collins

This expanded and updated edition first published
in Great Britain in 2009 by Bantam Press
an imprint of Transworld Publishers
Bantam edition published 2010

Copyright © Anthony Bourke and John Rendall 1971, 2009
Photographs © Derek Cattani, the Born Free Foundation, GAWPT and Bill Travers

Anthony Bourke and John Rendall have asserted their right under the Copyright,
Designs and Patents Act 1988 to be identified as the authors of this work.

Foreword and letter by George Adamson reproduced with the kind permission of
Tony Fitzjohn at GAWPT.
Letter by Bill Travers reproduced with the kind permission of Will Travers and
Virginia McKenna at the Born Free Foundation.

This book is a work of non-fiction based on the lives, experiences and recollections
of Anthony Bourke and John Rendall. In some limited cases names of people,
places, dates, sequences or the detail of events have been changed to protect the
privacy of others. The authors have stated to the publishers that, except in such
minor respects, the contents of this book are true.

A CIP catalogue record for this book
is available from the British Library.

Addresses for Random House Group Ltd companies outside the UK
can be found at: www.randomhouse.co.uk
The Random House Group Ltd Reg. No. 954009

The Random House Group Limited supports The Forest Stewardship Council
(FSC), the leading international forest certification organisation. All our titles that
are printed on Greenpeace approved FSC certified paper carry the FSC logo. Our
paper procurement policy can be found at www.rbooks.co.uk/environment

Typeset in Minion by Falcon Oast Graphic Art.
Printed in the UK by CPI Cox & Wyman, Reading, RG1 8EX.

2 4 6 8 10 9 7 5 3 1

To Christian, and our families who never met him.

Contents

Acknowledgements

IN THE 1971 EDITION of *A Lion Called Christian* we thanked the people who had helped make Christian's life with us in England both possible and happy, and those who helped return him to the wild.

In London: Roy Hazle, the buyer for the pet department at Harrods, and Sandy Lloyd; Jennifer-Mary Taylor, Joe Harding and John Barnardiston, the owners of Sophistocat, the pine furniture shop where Christian lived in the King's Road; Kay Dew; our accepting neighbours in the World's End; the Reverend H. R. and Mrs Williamson and Joan and Rod Thomas at the Moravian Close; Christian's best friend Unity Bevis-Jones; Amelia Nathan; and Bill Travers and Virginia McKenna, who introduced us to George Adamson.

In Nairobi: Monty Ruben, Jack Block, Agneta von Rosen, Ulf and Marianne Aschan, and the Ministry of

ACKNOWLEDGEMENTS

Wildlife and Tourism, who agreed to Christian's rehabilitation at Kora.

At Kampi ya Simba, Kora, north of Garissa on the Tana River: George Adamson; his engineer and road-builder brother Terence; Tony Fitzjohn; their staff Stanley and Hamisi Farah; George's lifelong friends Nevil Baxendale and his son Jonny (George's godson); the Provincial Game Warden of Garissa Ken Smith; veterinarian Dr Sue Harthoorn, cameraman Simon Trevor, and the Tana River Council.

At Collins the original publisher: Sir William Collins and our then editor Adrian House, Derek Cattani for his photographs in England and Kenya, and Toni Rendall and Mandy Barrett, who typed our original manuscript.

Sadly some of these key people are no longer alive today, including Sir William Collins, George Adamson and Bill Travers. George would have enjoyed the revival of interest in his work with lions and Christian's life. The George Adamson Wildlife Preservation Trust continues to fund major conservation projects in George's memory.

ACKNOWLEDGEMENTS

Thanks also to Caroline Michel, Alexandra Henderson, Lauren Miller Cilento, Pat Bourke and Lindy Bourke, and Sally Gaminara for their help and advice in the production of this book.

Anthony ('Ace') Bourke and John Rendall
2009

Foreword

by George Adamson

IN APRIL 1970, I received a letter from London from my friend Bill Travers, telling me about 'Christian', a fifth generation English lion, and asking whether I would be prepared to take him over and rehabilitate him back to the wild of his forebears. The idea appealed to me greatly, not only because it would save Christian from a lifetime of captivity, but also because it would be in all probability the first time an English lion had been returned to the life for which he was created.

I felt confident that his inherited knowledge and instincts would soon assert themselves, given the chance, and in spite of his breeding. I must admit that I did not feel the same confidence about his two owners, when I heard that they would accompany Christian and stay a few weeks at my camp. I was led to believe they were very 'mod' with long hair and exotic clothing. My first sight at Nairobi Airport of pink bell-bottomed trousers and flowing locks did nothing to dispel my misgivings. But Ace and John soon restored my faith in the modern generation. Immediately, I sensed the bond of deep affection and trust between them and Christian. I know from experience how hard it must have been for them to leave Christian to face the inevitable dangers and hardships confronting a lion in the wild.

At the time of writing, Christian is nearly two years old. He is as much at home in this wilderness as if he had been born here. Apart from initial toughening up, he required no training. Always the wonderful store-house of inherited knowledge has shown him the way.

Kampi ya Simba, Kora
15 July 1971

Introduction

IN 1971 WE WROTE *A Lion Called Christian*, the story of a lion from London who returned to Africa. And now, forty years later, the Internet's YouTube has introduced Christian to a new world audience, who are intrigued and enchanted by his extraordinary story.

We were two young travellers from Australia who had just arrived in London, and unexpectedly bought a lion cub from Harrods department store. We lived with him in London, then in the country, until it was arranged for him to be returned to Kenya and rehabilitated by George Adamson of *Born Free* fame.

Two documentaries, *The Lion at World's End* and *Christian the Lion*, were made about George Adamson assembling a pride of lions, centred on Christian's return to the wild. The YouTube clip features our unforgettable reunion with a now much bigger lion on our return to Kenya one year later in 1971.

We are both proud of the 1971 edition of this book, written when we were in our early twenties, and this revised and updated edition remains true to the original text. However, we took the opportunity to add new information and make some clarifications, and in some instances we have tried to express ourselves more effectively.

Forty years later some of our memories are very vivid, and some are vaguer. We have consulted two very good books referring to Christian which have been published subsequently: George Adamson's 1986 autobiography *My Pride and Joy*, and Adrian House's 1993 *The Great Safari: The Lives of George and Joy Adamson*. These books verified the chronology of some particular events for us, and provided new information. Another source was the letters Ace wrote to his parents from this period that until recently he was unaware had been kept. The first edition of *A Lion Called Christian* concluded in 1970, and this new edition has been updated to include our visits to Christian in 1971 and in 1972.

The book is being republished in response to the great interest in Christian's story generated by the

YouTube clip of our 1971 reunion. In April 2007 we began receiving emails alerting us that the reunion footage was on YouTube. We did not know who posted it, and we would not have known how to do it ourselves even if we had thought of it. We recently located Lisa Williams, a young art student from Los Angeles who posted the original footage (without audio) on YouTube late in 2006. We did not really monitor the interest, but in early 2008 we noticed the clip was becoming more popular. It was being sent around the world as one of those 'send this on to someone you love' emails complete with Whitney Houston's version of the highly emotive 'I Will Always Love You' as the backing track which had been added in early 2007. The hits on YouTube began to climb into the millions and other sites opened. We occasionally read the comments but felt like voyeurs into our own lives. Most people found the clip extremely moving and comments were very positive, which is apparently uncommon and was often remarked on by other commentators. It was a very special experience that we now all shared.

The Internet is unregulated territory, and quite a

lot of the information about Christian and us was incorrect, particularly the suggestion that we were in danger when we went back to see Christian. George had then known Christian for a year, and he was confident he would recognize us and greet us, although he admitted later that he did not expect such an exuberant display of affection.

Late in 2008 the American television host Ellen DeGeneres showed the clip on her programme, and invited Virginia McKenna and John to appear. They were unavailable, but the showing of the reunion clip saw the hits on the site climb to three million, and led to many other international television broadcasts. Christian had become world news, and we stopped counting as the hits reached sixty million, and the sites expanded to over eight hundred. Hollywood producers began to call. Funny spoofs and parodies have since been posted, and another unknown person joined Christian to Facebook, where he now has many friends.

Christian's story was well known in 1971. The book was published in four languages and serialized in many magazines. The documentaries *The Lion at World's End* and *Christian the Lion* were repeatedly shown on television in many countries. Then, naturally, the interest gradually faded, and as the years passed the memory of the experience seemed to us like a secret dream, a fantasy or even a hallucination.

Last time, in the early 1970s, people were aware of the entire story – the novelty of a London lion returning to Africa. But this time, because of those few filmed minutes of our 1971 reunion in the clip, the focus has been on the loving relationship we had with a rapidly growing, supposedly wild animal, and the extraordinary welcome we received from him after a year. The interest and the thoughtful responses have been overwhelming for us, and have given us the opportunity to reflect on the experience so many years later. One emailer, Joanna C. Avery, felt that we were able to overcome the stereotypes that society imposes on animals and bridge the differences between us to reveal our similarities.

We have tried to understand why the clip has struck such an emotional chord with millions of people. Is it the unconditional love Christian demonstrated? Is it about growing up and separation? Is it about loss and loneliness and the joy of reconnection? Are people projecting their own feelings and needs in relation to their own animals, and the solace and companionship they provide? With the domination of technology and computer games replacing outdoor activities, are we all now too alienated from the natural world? Is it nostalgia for a time when childhood was more carefree and safer, with more freedom and time for youthful adventures?

The Internet has revolutionized communication and offers still unimaginable opportunities for social networking, entertainment and information dissemination as well as social and political activism. Through the Internet we can now exert real influence on causes we believe in. We wonder what we could all achieve together if we worked in concert to address some of the world's most urgent social, environmental and wildlife issues.

1

A Lion with a Price Tag

NO ZOO IS COMPLETE without lions. The small zoo at Ilfracombe in Devon in the south-west of England was no exception, and the lion and lioness were a particularly handsome pair. The lion had been bought from the Rotterdam Zoo in Holland, and the lioness had come from the Biblical Zoo in Jerusalem. They had their first litter on 12 August 1969; four healthy cubs, one male and three females. Nine weeks later, with summer over and no more holiday crowds to attract, two female cubs were sent to an animal dealer and were subsequently bought by a circus. The remaining female and male were bought by Harrods, the Knightsbridge department store, and sent to London by train. The four cubs seemed destined, as their parents were, for a lifetime of frustration and confinement.

Three months before the cubs were born, we had left Australia for the first time, uncertain but optimistic.

We had both graduated from university and had had a variety of jobs with no clear career path at that stage. We headed to London as many young Australians had before us, and well-known examples include the satirist Barry Humphries, journalist and broadcaster Clive James, academic and writer Germaine Greer, artists Sidney Nolan, Brett Whiteley and Martin Sharp, social commentator Richard Neville, and more recently Kylie Minogue. Some Australians travelled overland through Asia and the Middle East, which is difficult if not impossible these days. We travelled independently for several months, but met up unexpectedly in London in late November 1969. We weren't exactly conscientious sightseers, but one day in an unusual burst of enthusiasm we visited, amongst other tourist destinations, the Tower of London. A suitable contrast, we decided, would be our first visit to Harrods. We were aware of Harrods' boast that they could provide anything, at a price of course. A friend had once enquired about a camel and been asked, 'Would that be with one hump or two?' But Harrods seemed to have extended themselves beyond our imagination, when on wandering into their zoo on the second floor we discovered two lion cubs in a small cage between the Siamese kittens and the old English sheep dogs. A lion cub with a price tag was not an easy thought to assimilate. The cubs were proving to be a successful drawcard for the Christmas shoppers, with the prospect of becoming the Christmas present for the person who already had everything.

We had not thought about lions before. Of course we had seen them in zoos, but that was as far as our interest and knowledge extended. Neither of us had even read Joy Adamson's 1960 book *Born Free*, the story of Elsa the lioness. She had been found as a cub, raised and rehabilitated back into the wild by Joy and her husband George Adamson, who was a game warden with the Kenyan Wildlife Department.

We sympathized with the cubs, for despite the efforts of the staff they were incessantly disturbed by intrigued shoppers, yet we had to restrain the same urge within ourselves. Each person demanded a response. The female snarled in an alarming manner and people were satisfied, but her brother pretended none of us existed. He was irresistible, and we sat, enchanted, beside their cage for hours.

John: 'Why don't we buy him?'

Ace: 'I've already named him Christian.'

We found out much later that the staff had named him Marcus, a handsome masculine name, but Christian seemed to suit him, and we liked the irony of Christians being fed to the lions in Roman times, which was also a reminder of the danger to which we could be exposing ourselves, and the people around us.

We intuitively knew that we were both serious, and a curious excitement began to grow. Even if it was only for a couple of months, surely we could offer him a better life than this, and try to ensure a better future for him? Or was it that we just wanted to take Christian away from everyone else, and have him to ourselves? Neither of us had ever fantasized about or dreamed of owning an exotic pet, but he was completely irresistible.

Suddenly our lives were to be incomplete without a lion cub. An impractical idea for two young Australians visiting Europe, but at least we could allow ourselves the luxury of investigating the possibility of buying him. We enquired if he was still for sale. The female had been sold, but the male was still available, for two hundred and fifty guineas, equivalent in 2009 to three thousand five hundred English pounds. This was a vast sum to us, but, undaunted, we nonchalantly agreed that it seemed a very reasonable price. The assistant at the zoo suggested we speak to the Harrods buyer. He was, she pointedly warned us, interviewing any prospective purchasers very thoroughly, as Harrods believed it was important the lions did not fall into irresponsible hands.

We returned the next morning looking far more respectable, with our hair skilfully flattened, and wearing the tweed sports coats our parents, very perceptively, had insisted would be useful abroad, but which until now had been lying untouched at the bottom of our suitcases. We succeeded, with the help of a few tiny white lies and our enthusiasm, in convincing Roy Hazle, the buyer for Harrods, that we would be responsible guardians/foster parents for a lion. Now, when Harrods was prepared to part with him, we had the first option to buy Christian.

Everything up to this point seemed very natural

and straightforward. We had gone shopping and had seen a lion that we liked and now wanted to buy, but could not take delivery for about three weeks. We shared a small flat on the King's Road in Chelsea, above the shop where we had both been offered work, and in all respects could not have been in a worse position to own any animal, least of all a lion. We spent days fruitlessly visiting estate agents, looking for a basement flat with a garden, 'for our dog'. It seemed pointless being truthful with them, when it was the landlords we would really have to contend with. We were becoming very disheartened, so we decided to advertise in *The Times* on the assumption that the courageous or eccentric landlord we had been unable to find would probably be a reader of this newspaper.

LION CUB, 2 young men seek suitable garden/roof,
flat/house London. 352 7252.

The only responses we received were a flood of telephone calls from other newspapers, prematurely wanting to photograph the lion.

In desperation, our last hope was to persuade the owners of the shop, Joe Harding, John Barnardiston and Jennifer-Mary Taylor, that in addition to us as employees, their business really needed a lion cub living on the premises, particularly as the shop was called Sophistocat. John Barnardiston was cautious by nature, being English, and fortunately in Switzerland at the time. Joe Harding was born in Kenya and had owned a variety of animals, and put up no opposition, and Jennifer-Mary was enthusiastic. It was decided that Christian would live in the basement of the shop, and it was to be a surprise for John on his return from Switzerland. As we would be living above the shop and working there, it seemed an ideal arrangement, for we could devote all the attention to Christian we realized would be necessary. Although Sophistocat had an enormous basement, with several rooms, we also needed to find a garden for his exercise.

Fortunately we had friends living in a studio only three hundred yards from the shop, with access to a most suitable garden. Fully enclosed, and covering three-quarters of an acre, it is still owned by the

Moravian Church. The minister was an ardent bird-watcher, but not prejudiced against extending his zoological interests, and very generously gave his permission for us to use the garden. As a result, we now felt able to assure Harrods that we could fulfil the practical requirements for owning a lion in London.

Of course, looking back now many years later, we should never have been allowed to buy a lion. We were naive about the risks, and were without any insurance cover. Since the enactment of the Endangered Species Act in 1973 in England Harrods have no longer traded in exotic animals, and now has the Harrods 'pet shop' as opposed to a 'zoo'. We now appreciate how purchasing wild or exotic animals only encourages further trafficking in them.

But while our excitement accelerated, we became increasingly concerned by our total ignorance of the sorts of problems that faced us. We had no realistic idea to what extent a lion could be domesticated, and were aware that we could be taking on an impossible and futile task. We had grown up in family households that loved animals, but this did not prepare us for what lay ahead.

Ace was brought up in Newcastle, a city to the north of Sydney in New South Wales. He lived on the edge of the bush, rode horses and always had dogs as pets, although at eleven years old he found his first cat in the vacant allotment next door. There were many family camping and fishing holidays to the coast and into the country.

John grew up in Bathurst, a major country town 130 miles inland from Sydney, where the family pets included cats, a number of tough kelpie cattle-dogs, and often young kangaroos that had been rescued when their mothers had either been shot as vermin or killed on the road. Rabbits were also considered vermin. They and their predator the fox are both examples of a disastrous importation of animals that has caused huge environmental damage to indigenous species and habitats.

At Harrods we were told that the cubs had been handled by humans since birth, and that they both, particularly Christian, were responding to affection. We were recently contacted by a former zoo staff member who informed us that Christian's mother had rejected the cubs and she had hand-reared Christian and his sister, so he had had early contact with humans. He was the favourite, and appeared to have a delightful, even-tempered nature. As often as we could, we went to Harrods to play with the cubs when they were let out of their cage for an hour after closing time. We wanted to spend as much time with him as possible, and it would make his transition to Sophistocat and the King's Road easier if he was familiar with us. Both cubs were excessively playful, and while it was possible to handle them, they could be quite uncontrollable at times. They had extremely sharp teeth, and claws which they had not yet learnt to control, and it was difficult to avoid being scratched. Christian was definitely more accepting than his sister, and we hoped he would be less boisterous and more manageable when he was separated from her.

Roy Hazle sensibly suggested that before we made our final decision to buy Christian, we talk to Charles Bewick and Peter Bowen, who had bought a puma from Harrods the year before. The puma, who was called Margot after a family friend Dame Margot Fonteyn, the prima ballerina, was now fully grown, and although she seemed to have adjusted to life in London, we never really felt at ease with her. We were assured that she had an impeccable behaviour record, and because Peter and Charles had been able to devote considerable time to her she was sufficiently domesticated to co-exist quite happily with them. It was encouraging, for they had obviously found the whole experience enjoyable, and much less complicated than they had anticipated.

We realized it was unlikely that we would be able to have Christian for more than about six months. He would rapidly outgrow any environment we could provide. We were determined to make those months as happy and as safe as we possibly could for him, but was it fair if he was then to go back to a zoo? Surely it would just make it harder for him, and the whole venture merely a marvellous indulgence for us. We decided to visit Longleat Safari Park in Wiltshire in the English countryside to see if it would be suitable for Christian. The park, the outcome of a partnership between the Marquis of Bath and Jimmy Chipperfield, the circus owner, had opened in 1966. It was the first safari park to open outside Africa, and was innovative in the care of animals, but controversial at the time as neighbours feared the lions might escape. We were aware that when it had first opened, basic assumptions about lions had proved incorrect, and the lions had suffered casualties. Now, with the park extending to over one hundred acres, and the lions divided into prides, they appeared to have created the best living conditions for lions in England. Roger Cawley, the manager, said he would be delighted to take Christian when he outgrew us.

Not only were we now in a position to have Christian, but we could also ensure that he would not spend the rest of his life in a zoo or in a circus. But still we both had very serious doubts. Were we really prepared to take on this enormous, binding responsibility? We could not ignore the fact that it was a lion, a basically wild animal and the most powerful predator after man, that we were bringing into our lives, and the lives of the people around us. We knew that a workable human/lion relationship was not an impossibility, but we could not be certain that we would attain this with Christian. He was now four months old and growing

'Fashion victims' Ace Bourke (left) and John Rendall on the King's Road with Christian in 1970.

Above: Easter 1970. 'And there were no casualties...'

Opposite page: Waste-paper baskets were first worn on the head, then destroyed.

Opposite page: In the flat above Sophistocat.

Left: Surveying his kingdom.

Below: His favourite position on the stairs at the shop.

Above: Football in the Moravian Close.

Opposite page: Christian, like all lions, was fascinated by children.

Christian was always curious, and could never resist an open drawer.

very quickly. Soon he would be capable of inflicting considerable damage. But while one of us talked of our recklessness and the risks, the other spoke of the unforgettable and exciting experience that lay ahead. What finally united us was the staunch opposition from most people we knew to the idea of buying Christian. Unwittingly they intensified our determination to accept a challenge we might otherwise have resisted. Our parents were no doubt horrified, but only cautioned us against a decision we might regret and that it would be difficult giving Christian up. It was a step into the unknown. We were young, we were looking for fun and adventure, and we had left Australia, our parents and some of our inhibitions behind. It was the tail-end of the historic 1960s and the beginning of the 1970s, a time of great social change, optimism and opportunities.

On 15 December 1969 we received a telephone call to say we could collect Christian unexpectedly a few days early. He and his sister had escaped into the adjoining carpet department in the middle of the night and destroyed some goatskin rugs that were part of a

Christmas display. We collected Christian the next day, walking him out through the staff exit on a lead. The staff waved goodbye, no doubt relieved that their responsibilities were over. With Christian sitting majestically and deceptively still on the back seat of the car, we drove off towards the King's Road, extremely happy and nervously excited, but with an unvoiced suspicion and fear that we had committed ourselves to something that could prove just too big for us.

2

Sophistocat

IT IS A SHORT DRIVE from Harrods in Knightsbridge to Sophistocat in Chelsea, but after his months in a cage Christian's world must have suddenly assumed the most enormous proportions. Frightened and confused when the car began to move, he scrambled all over us, and we had to stop frequently, having no idea how we could begin to control him. We tried to placate him with a huge teddy bear that we had bought him as a welcoming present, but his total lack of interest in it left us helpless. Eventually we arrived at Sophistocat, where friends impatiently waited. We carried him into the shop, and Christian, now much calmer, padded around investigating everything, and cleverly evaded all the hands that tentatively and incredulously reached down to pat him. He seemed only mildly disorientated, and focused most of his attention on us. Having spent time with him at Harrods after hours, we presumably represented the only link with his immediate past. We stayed up most of the night playing with him. Christian was ours.

A resident lion in the King's Road, Chelsea, was not too surprising at the time. In the 1960s London had become a Mecca for designers, musicians, artists, photographers and writers, plus many other creative people and hangers-on, who were all part of 'Swinging London'. The Beatles, David Bowie and the Rolling Stones were familiar sights around Chelsea. Fashion designers of the time included Mary Quant, Barbara Hulanicki at Biba, Zandra Rhodes, Ossie Clark and Michael Fish. Exotic animals were part of this quite glamorous mix: in addition to Margot the puma we knew of a serval cat that lived nearby, while the casino owner John Aspinall kept tigers and gorillas. For a mile from Sloane Square, the King's Road was scattered with trendy clothes shops, restaurants, clubs and antique markets. The façade was ephemeral, but the basic character remained the same: superficial and pretentious, but great fun and not without attraction. Every Saturday the road was blocked by a self-conscious parade of people and expensive cars. Tourists came to watch, while the others, in beautiful or flamboyant clothes, came to be watched. While the clothes were fun to wear at the time, in retrospect most of us were fashion victims, and we view the more recent revisiting of 1970s retro fashion with amused embarrassment.

Sophistocat sold antique pine furniture, and was situated in a curious area called the World's End, which historically marked the point where King Charles II's Road and protection from highwaymen ended – a raffish tradition that lingered on. A long way down the King's Road, the World's End was becoming part of fashionable Chelsea, and the locals resented the growing intrusion of a few smart antique and clothes shops, which included Nigel Weymouth's 'Granny Takes a Trip' and Vivienne Westwood and Malcolm McLaren's boutique, then called 'Seditionaries', later 'Sex', and now 'World's End'. Punk music and clothes would soon emerge from our grungier end of the King's Road.

Within two days Christian seemed to have fully adjusted to his new surroundings. Any initial inhibitions had vanished, and the teddy bear was already in a million pieces. He obviously enjoyed his greater freedom in this large two-level shop, and was much less boisterous without his sister. There was no indication that he missed her. Perhaps we were some form of substitute; and, having none of the indifference common to most cats, he wanted to be near us. Lions are not as disdainful as other cats, and are more dog-like in their sociability. Lions simply *know* they are number one and just assume superiority. Now four months old, thirty pounds, and about two feet long, he was himself a larger-than-life teddy bear. He loved being carried and cuddled, and his paws would gently reach round our necks and his tongue lick our faces. He had soft, tawny-coloured fur, and was surprisingly heavily spotted. Although he was well co-ordinated, his paws, head and ears were disproportionately large for the rest of his body, giving an indication of the size and strength of the animal he would grow into. But it was his beautiful, round, rust-coloured eyes that dominated his appearance. He had a delightful, placid nature, and was so easy to manage that we felt we had over-dramatized the problems of owning a lion. He was even house-trained.

With the fastidiousness of all cats, he and his sister had used the same corner of their cage at Harrods, so we were optimistic. In one of the rooms in the basement we had installed a heater and put blankets for him to sleep on. In a corner we placed an improvised lion-sized kitty litter tray. After two days of indiscriminate puddles and messes, which we followed each time by a smack and then carrying him to the tray, the problem was solved. He quickly learnt his name, and 'no'. It all seemed too easy.

He was adaptable, and responsive to routine. His day began about 8 a.m. when one of us came downstairs. Although it seemed unnatural, quite often he had to be woken, and a sleepy, blinking little lion would affectionately greet us, and walk unsteadily over to squat on his tray. Then it was time to be fed. His first and last meals of the day were a mixture of baby foods: Complan, Farex, and milk, with Abidec drops for additional vitamins. Sandy Lloyd, the assistant at Harrods Zoo, had adored the cubs and looked after them extremely well, and she provided us with a carefully balanced diet sheet for Christian. Two main meals, given to him late in the morning and in the early evening, consisted of three-quarters of a pound of raw meat, a raw egg, and a spoonful of bone meal to prevent a calcium deficiency. We varied the meat and occasionally gave him an unskinned rabbit. Christian always carried the skin around Sophistocat for several days until it finally disintegrated or the smell became too overwhelming. He enjoyed having huge bones to play with and gnaw, and as there was no competition from other animals, we could safely handle his food as he ate.

We were to find that people's preconceptions about lions were often wrong. For example, it is a fallacy that it is dangerous to give an animal such as a lion raw meat because it supposedly will turn them into 'man-eaters'. We rather enviously eyed the delicious fillet steaks that a French chef sometimes brought in for Christian. The chef loved lions and of course had access to plentiful supplies of meat. The quantity of meat Christian required increased weekly, and he became so expensive to feed that we regretted not being able to turn him into a vegetarian!

He was inexhaustibly playful and had a variety of

toys and rubber balls scattered all over the shop and the basement. Wastepaper baskets were a great favourite, first to be worn on the head, totally obscuring his sight, and then to be ripped apart. We had to buy him hardy toys, for the average life of a normal teddy bear was about two minutes. He demanded our constant attention and it was impossible to ignore him. If one of us was reading a newspaper, or on the telephone, Christian would immediately climb up on to his lap. Sophistocat was a jungle of furniture, and he incessantly stalked us through it, becoming expert at creating games. He knew we would not allow him to jump on us, but he would cleverly manoeuvre himself into position behind a piece of furniture, so that it appeared as if we were in fact temptingly hiding from him. Then with a clear conscience he would charge and leap at us. We developed a habit of glancing nervously over our shoulders. If we caught him frozen in a crouched position with intent mischievous eyes, he would nonchalantly pretend to clean his paws, rather irritated that his fun had been spoiled, for the game was to stalk and catch us unawares. Very quickly we could usually predict what his intentions were from the expression in his eyes. He was always entertaining and amusing, but very exhausting and demanding.

When we played with him we discouraged him from being too boisterous or getting over-excited, and we did not wrestle roughly with him, or encourage him to chase us. We never let him realize that at a certain point he had become physically stronger than us, and could harm us. We avoided and ignored any overt demonstrations of his superior strength. Sometimes while playing, if he had us in an awkward or 'alpha' position on the ground, he would instinctively sense his advantage and get a surge of energy and determination which alarmed us and seemed to mystify him.

He looked forward each morning to the arrival of Kay Dew, the daily cleaner, for he was certain that she had been provided for his enjoyment. He chased her brooms, rode on the vacuum cleaner, and stole or ate her dusters. She handled him very well, but warily watched the Farex and Complan smudges grow higher on the windows and glass doors.

When Christian first came to the King's Road, he

was small enough to run around the shop with our customers. They rarely took seriously our initial warning, 'Do you have any objection to lions?' One disbelieving woman, on seeing one of Christian's bones, said, 'That bone is at least lion-sized.' 'That's what we tried to tell you. Look behind you.' She watched incredulously as Christian ambled past to claim his bone. Usually it was good for business, and the owners of Sophistocat were incredibly tolerant. Even the English had to react to a lion cub stretched out on the antique pine table they were contemplating buying. Most people were delighted, and no one complained about the occasional laddered stockings or torn trousers. Many women customers returned with sceptical husbands and friends, and carloads of children on Saturdays, which were busy anyway with the usual King's Road Parade, and Sophistocat suddenly acquired an unwelcome zoo- or circus-like atmosphere. To dispel this, Christian had to spend most of the day in the basement, and only the particularly disappointed, or the particularly attractive, could persuade us to take them downstairs to see him.

Every afternoon he went to the garden in the nearby Moravian Close for exercise. Harrods had given us a collar and lead for him and while the collar looked incongruous it was necessary, as it made it easier to hold him, and he quickly forgot about it. At first we tried to walk him to the garden on his lead, as it was only three hundred yards. But he never walked, just sprinted for a little way and then resolutely sat down. He was frightened of the traffic, and the people who crowded around him. We dreaded meeting other animals, for although he did not appear overly interested in them he found them a welcome diversion. For the first few weeks we could just pick him up and carry him, but he soon grew much heavier, and the short walk became an ordeal. While it would have been easier if he had walked on the lead, it was unfair to expect such unnatural behaviour from a lion, so we did not persist, and resorted to driving him there in the car, or in the Sophistocat van. He was always manageable in both, but restless, as lions can never fully accept any form of restriction.

The garden was ideal. No humans, no animals, and

surrounded by a high brick wall. This wall dates from the Tudor period, and the present studios and the old Moravian chapel in the garden are built on the foundations of Sir Thomas More's stables. After a succession of eminent owners, Sir Hans Sloane sold the property in 1750 to Count Zinzendorf of Saxony, who bought the land to found a Moravian settlement in England. The Moravians were among the first independent Protestants and had formed their brotherhood in 1457 when they protested against the moral corruption and political activity of the Roman Catholic Church in Bohemia. They take the name Moravians, rather than Bohemians, from the group of refugees from Moravia who settled on Count Zinzendorf's estate in Saxony in 1722. The count's son, Christian Renatus, Count of Zinzendorf and Pottendorf, is buried in the garden. Actually it is a graveyard but the Moravians bury their dead very unostentatiously – vertically, with modest horizontal headstones – so this was not at all obvious. Looking back, we do feel a little guilty about playing in a graveyard.

There was a large area of grass for Christian to play

on, and trees and hedges to hide behind. Interestingly, it took several weeks for him to adjust to all the space, and initially he would not go out into the centre of the garden, away from the protection of the hedges. But then the garden became his established territory, and he adored it. He loved chasing and jumping on us, but we thought this was an inadvisable habit to encourage in a lion, so we kicked footballs for him to chase instead. He was remarkably fast, and beautifully co-ordinated. He would run after the ball, pounce on it, and dramatically roll over and over with it. The few times there was snow, he loved skidding through it, and was not worried by the cold. We spent about an hour each day at the garden, which seemed adequate, for he was rarely reluctant to return to Sophistocat. Besides, it was time for his favourite entertainment.

Late in the afternoon Christian would sit regally on the furniture in the shop window, in the spotlight, watching the activities of the World's End. He was the area's star attraction, and the locals, particularly the children, loved him and were very proud of him. He seemed to belong to all of them. In the window he drew appreciative crowds of regular admirers or astonished newcomers. These were happy hours. If there were too many people and his view was obscured, he simply changed windows. Several motorists, seeing Christian unselfconsciously displaying himself, bumped into the cars in front. And a conversation was overheard between a child and his mother on a passing bus: 'Mummy, there was a lion in that shop window!' 'Don't be ridiculous. If you don't stop this lying, I'll get your father to thrash you.'

3

Noblesse Oblige

WE HAD NOT TOLD Christian that he was a lion. We thought this knowledge would only lead to regrettable lion-like behaviour. We avoided using the word 'lion' in front of him, but occasionally had to spell out L-I-O-N to people who thought Christian was a leopard because of his spots. He enjoyed looking at himself in the large mirrors at Sophistocat, so while he must have been confused as to what sort of animal he was, he knew exactly what he looked like. He often accompanied us in the car, and as there are possibly more sculptured lions in London than there are live ones in Africa we decided to tell him the truth, before he discovered it himself and asked awkward questions. We drove him to Trafalgar Square to see the lions at the base of Nelson's Column. He was delighted to be such an obvious symbol of nobility. Fortunately the information did not alter his behaviour, for he had like all cats assumed superiority over us from the beginning. But too much knowledge could be dangerous or confusing, so we asked the Moravian minister not to tell him that the early Christians had been fed to the lions.

Consistent with their standards, Harrods had sold us a lion of quality. He was very healthy and had a beautiful nature. He was even-tempered, and not easily alarmed or frightened. These qualities were reinforced by his trust in us and his strong feeling of security. The fact that his behaviour was in general quite predictable and consistent made living with him much easier than it could have been. We navigated our way very carefully with him, getting to know him and learning about him quickly. We rarely misjudged his intentions, and learnt to anticipate any situations that could have unpredictable outcomes.

It was easy to recognize a psychological pattern of behaviour in him which could be interpreted in human terms. While we accept this is anthropomorphic, to us aspects of his personality did resemble a human's personality. His 'sense of humour' seemed very similar to ours. If he tripped over something, and with his huge paws he tended to be rather clumsy for a lion, he appeared 'embarrassed' but would quickly pretend, as most people do, that nothing had happened. It seemed lions can communicate with humans much more closely than almost any other animal. We were realizing that the two most powerful predators in the world have much in common.

Christian's personality was immense, and his presence entirely filled the shop and our lives. We realized that if the months he was to live with us were to be as happy for him as we intended, he had to be allowed as much natural expression as possible. For him to remain the contented, even-tempered animal he was, it was necessary, in addition to giving him all the time and affection we had, to minimize any restriction.

We attained a relationship of mutual respect, with no hint from him of domestic-animal subservience. We made no attempt to dominate or train him, and in our experience this would probably have had disastrous consequences. It is doubtful if a lion can ever be totally dominated; perhaps precarious control is the most that can be achieved. And a lion's respect is not easily earned. Christian had a determined character, but he seemed to realize that he had to co-operate, and he quickly knew what sort of behaviour would not be allowed. Neither of us has had any contact with circus animals or animals used in live entertainment. One can only guess at the psychological games, bribes, rewards and punishments involved in getting animals to perform. In 2003 Roy, half of the Las Vegas double act Siegfried and Roy, was attacked by one of his tigers during an animal illusionist performance.

Christian hated being ignored, and was very conscious of the effect he had on humans. He could not resist testing the reactions of newcomers, and always remembered if people had not coped well with him previously. Like all animals he always knew when someone was uncomfortable around him, and would take advantage of this. If customers had not noticed him sitting on the stairs in the shop, he would grunt to attract their attention. From this commanding position, his paws knocked off several hats and pairs of glasses. He was extremely curious, and his eyes were always watching and searching for anything new that ought to be investigated.

It was his eyes that were his most arresting feature. They were expressive, intelligent eyes that could transmit love and trust, or challenge or defy us. Sometimes they had incredible clarity and brightness but sometimes they could be opaque, unknowable and impenetrable, and stare straight through us to a dimension beyond, from which we were excluded.

Christian possessed a memory for people and places, and demonstrated a high degree of intelligence compared to other lions we subsequently met. He quickly learnt how to open the door of the basement if it was not locked. We kept his food for the day on the top of various cupboards in the office at the back of the shop, and he frequently managed the complicated business of climbing high enough on other furniture to be able to stand up on his hind legs and knock his food to the floor.

Unlike most other members of the cat family, lions are gregarious and social animals living in an extended family pride. Christian undoubtedly regarded us as his family, and was tremendously affectionate towards us. Lions greet each other with a ceremonial touching of heads, and we often knelt to enable him to do this with us. Any parting from him, regardless of its duration, involved another fond greeting, a lick and a cuddle. He enjoyed being close, often either leaning against us, or actually sitting on us. Sometimes he would dramatically leap from the ground into our arms, which was a greeting for us that no one had ever seen before in lions. Of course he could be arrogant and demanding, but if he had to be disciplined, either verbally or with a smack, he accepted it, and did not bear any resentment. He was very much aware when we were displeased with him, and if he felt it was deserved he would make obvious and usually successful attempts to win us over again.

Christian was particularly unaggressive and unpossessive about his food, which indicated that in some respects he was an exceptional lion. He had no other animals to compete with, and this, together with the knowledge that he was fed regularly, must have been a contributing factor. But people who knew a great deal more about lions than we did were always astounded by his attitude towards his food. He had a healthy appetite, and in his eagerness he often knocked his food out of our hands before we had time to place it on the floor for him. But we could take his food away from him if it was necessary, even out of his mouth. He loved the marrow inside bones, but as he was unable to get it out he gently ate it from the tips of our fingers.

Lions depend to a large extent on their mouths for communication and contact. He licked us to show his affection. His rough tongue always tested surfaces for their taste and texture. He had sharp milk teeth, and while he enjoyed mouthing our hands and arms, he quickly learnt not to bite us. There were moods, however, in which his mouth just hung open, waiting to be filled. Kneecaps were a suitable height. Our clothes were often damaged when his teeth or claws got caught, and we sometimes resorted to wearing practical bottle-green boiler suits.

A lion needs to exercise his claws and jaws. In the first few weeks, several table and chair legs in the shop were damaged. However, after a few smacks he gave this up, especially when he realized he could use the banisters on the stairs instead, for lions are creatures of habit. They are earth-bound in comparison with other cats, and he did not jump all over the furniture. But he enjoyed surveying his domain from a height, and would often sit on tables and chests of drawers. Fortunately, he preferred the stairs, which gave him greater height, and he would sit with a paw dangling elegantly over the side. Actually he damaged very little furniture, and then only if he slipped and dug his claws in for support. One day, rather unwisely, a very expensive table had been elaborately set with cutlery, china, glasses and candles in the middle of the shop. We heard the sound of breaking glass, and immediately knew what had happened. Confused by the unfamiliar display, Christian had moved his weight to one side of the table, and he and the tabletop had crashed to the floor. The table had been sold, and now there were several deep scratches on it. We telephoned the woman who had bought it to apologize. 'Don't worry,' she said. 'I only came into the shop to see Christian; the table was an afterthought. Please don't worry about the scratches. They will remind me of that beautiful lion.' But he could never resist attacking the mattress on a brass bed we were trying to sell. This problem was only solved when a friend very generously brought Christian a mattress of his own, and, wildly excited, like a lion with a kill, he expertly dragged it down to the basement, although it was much bigger and heavier than him.

He had formidably sharp claws, and before he learnt to retract them we received many scratches. Quite quickly he developed more control over them, and he also realized that we stopped playing with him if we were scratched. He learnt to keep them sheathed, but if he was wrestling with something such as his mattress, pretending it was a zebra he had just stalked and thrown to the ground, we had to remember that his claws would instinctively be out.

Like all lions Christian was fascinated by children. He seemed to consider them a different species from adults, and reacted differently to them. We were always extremely careful to hold him if children were in the shop. One day a photographer from a local newspaper was taking a photograph of him, on a leash, outside Sophistocat. A woman, probably thinking Christian was a dog, strode in front of him with her two-year-old child, also on a leash. Christian curiously extended one paw, and knocked the child to the pavement. One of us grabbed Christian while the other obscured the photographer from the sort of photograph the newspapers crave. The child was slightly dazed, but so swaddled with clothes it could not possibly have been hurt. At first the mother was furious, but as she returned later with endless friends, and other children to dangle in front of him, it was clear that she had quickly recovered and was apparently delighted with the incident.

Christian grew very quickly. Within two months the beginnings of a mane developed and he suddenly looked quite adult. It was unfair, and probably unwise, to expect innocent customers to cope with the experience of being sprung upon from behind a chest of drawers and clasped around their thighs by a lion's huge paws. He left most people alone, but like many other animals he instinctively identified those who were frightened, and he enjoyed teasing them. Obviously we could not risk any incidents, and no insurance company was prepared to cover us.

We began to feel the weight of the responsibility of

owning Christian. Chelsea football ground is nearby and the police visited us to advise that on match days Christian should not be allowed in the windows as this could provoke disturbances among the passing football supporters. He had to spend much more time in the basement, and was only permitted in the shop when there were no customers. He enjoyed being down there, and he had many toys to play with, but he resented not having the freedom to come up to the shop when he wished. Sometimes he would unnecessarily squat on his kitty litter tray, as an unsubtle sign that he was ready to go upstairs. Like all cats, lions are happy to sleep if there is nothing better to do, but his hours in the basement were broken by many visits. The others at Sophistocat, Joe, John and Jennifer-Mary, adored Christian, and he was just as fond of them. Usually at least one of us would be downstairs playing with him. When people came to see him we took them to the basement where it was easier for us to be in complete control of the situation, and if necessary prevent him from jumping on them. He was an unusually accepting lion and there were very few people he disliked. It was difficult to discover what he objected to; sometimes it might have been a strong perfume or an aftershave lotion, and he always jumped up on one friend of ours whenever he wore a particular coat.

We tried to keep Christian unaware of just how much – or how little – control we had over him. After the first few months it took him a surprisingly long time to realize that although we could still just carry him, if he struggled we had to release him immediately. If he played too roughly with us, we always stopped, and because of this he never knew he had passed the point where he had in fact become physically stronger than we were. For a lion he was very obedient, and he usually co-operated with us. Only rarely would he ignore our remonstrations, but when this happened there was very little we could do. We just had to pretend that we were not worried by what he was doing, rather than let him know that we could not stop him. It was a fascinating psychological game, but the stakes were high.

Lions give extremely clear and fair warnings of their displeasure. With their strength, teeth, and claws, it would be foolish to disregard them. Only once in the months that Christian lived at Sophistocat were we very frightened of him. He found a fur belt that had dropped off a coat, and ran down with it into the basement. We followed him to retrieve it. He was chewing the belt and making excited sucking sounds. We knew that this would be something he would be reluctant to give up. We tried to take it from him, but he flattened his ears and snarled a ferocious warning. He was an unrecognizable, wild animal. Undoubtedly he would have attacked us if we had tried again to take the belt from him. We wanted to leave him, but instead we slowly moved a few yards away, talking to one another as if nothing had happened, and we had forgotten about the belt. We knew we must not convey to him how frightened we were. It could have encouraged him to repeat the performance if he had sensed how effective it was. After about five minutes his excitement over the belt, and his anger, subsided. We spent the next few hours talking and playing with him very normally. We respected him for his distinct warning. The incident was never repeated, but we had been given an important reminder of Christian's potential danger.

4

'The Publicity-Shy
Jungle King'

WHEN THE LADY MAYOR of Kensington and Chelsea
came into Sophistocat to meet Christian and
bent over to stroke him, her elaborate chain of office
dangled temptingly in front of him. He could not resist,
and a large paw went out and swiped at it. The chain
whirled round her neck. She was dazed but unhurt.
Lions, monarchs by birth, are not impressed by the
trappings of municipal office.

A diverse assortment of people met Christian, and
some of them visited him regularly. One woman came
into the shop with jelly babies for the bear she had
heard lived there. She was greatly disappointed to find
that Christian was only a lion, and, worse, was not
tempted by the jelly babies. Actresses Diana Rigg and
Mia Farrow, customers at Sophistocat, loved meeting
him and came back to play with him. As Christian
received considerable publicity, several people came

into the shop concerned that we were just using him as a gimmick, but they were placated to see him so happy and healthy, and apparently very fond of us.

Having a lion became part of our lives and we had to accept all the interest he aroused. If we were not with him we were continually being asked about him. We had to listen patiently to people's stories of their 'wild' cats, while others reminisced about their experiences in Africa. We were constantly asked, 'How long will it be before he becomes a man-eater?' It was impossible to relate such questions to Christian, especially when watching him play with his best friend, Unity Bevis-Jones.

Unity met Christian in January 1970, one month after we had bought him. She heard that a lion lived at Sophistocat, and rushed immediately to the shop. She visited Christian every afternoon, and her life revolved around him. She was so slight we were worried that he would unintentionally hurt her, but she handled him extremely well. She wore a thick coat and a rather mad felt hat for protection. The hat obscured most of her face, and it was only when Christian finally ate it several

John (left) and Ace with Christian on the stairs to the flat.

John (left), Christian and Ace, in the showroom at Sophistocat.

Lunch with model Emma Breeze at the Casserole Restaurant on the King's Road, Chelsea.

Above: Christian with Mark at Todd's Hairdressers in the World's End.

Opposite page: In the flat above Sophistocat.

Left: Radio presenter Jack de Manio tries to interview Christian for Radio 4, but he failed to 'roar' for the listeners.

Below: Christian meets Virginia McKenna and Bill Travers.

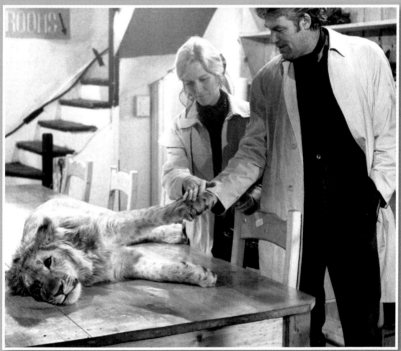

Watching out for customers
at Sophistocat.

Playing hide-and-seek in the Moravian Close.

weeks later that we realized how attractive she was.

Unity was addicted to lions. One day in Rome, where she was working as an actress, she had decided that she wanted a lion, although she had not known any before. She managed to persuade the Rome zoo to sell her a nine-month-old lioness that had just arrived at the zoo from Africa, and had never been handled by humans before. It did not occur to Unity that lions were something to be frightened of. After Lola was delivered in a crate, she was surprised when her flatmate locked herself in her bedroom for a fortnight. Unity found landlords just as unreasonable, and she estimated that in the year and a half she and Lola lived together they moved about twenty times. When Unity had to return to England, Lola went to live with friends near Naples. Unity had an extraordinary affinity with Christian, and we could understand how she had managed to have a successful and accident-free relationship with Lola, under much more difficult circumstances.

Each afternoon when Unity arrived at Sophistocat, Christian could be heard in the basement, noisily playing football with something, usually a plastic bucket. At the sound of her footsteps on the stairs, he would stop playing and listen and wait to see who it was. Unity would say: 'Hello, Christian, it's me.' Christian would grunt loudly, his normal greeting, and jump up at the locked door, to peer at her through a small round hole. To prevent him from running upstairs when she opened the door, Unity would ask Christian to move away before she came in. Still close to the door, he would indicate with a lion-like meow that it was safe for her to come in. 'No,' she would say, 'that's not far enough. Go further away.' After a brief silence, Christian would grunt, and if the grunt sounded sufficiently distant to Unity's experienced ears she would go in and shut the door behind her. Christian would rush to greet her fondly and, grabbing her by the coat, would enthusiastically lead her around the basement.

If he was too boisterous, and ignored her when she said 'Don't be too rough' or 'Stop it, Christian', she would edge towards the door when he was not looking, and leave him. Christian would run to the door and meow and grunt. We would hear Unity say, 'You're very naughty, and if you don't behave I'm not coming in to play with you. I'm not a bucket, and I don't expect to be treated like one.' As an apology, a few sorrowful grunts would follow, getting further and further from the door, to show Unity she could come in without his rushing upstairs. Reprimanded, but always forgiven, he would now be gentle with her, and they would entertain each other with games and conversation for the rest of the afternoon.

One of Christian's most endearing characteristics was that he had individual relationships with all of us; only subtle differences, but different greetings, different games and tricks, and he knew exactly what each of us would let him get away with. Unity could never bring herself to refuse him anything. She often came to the garden with us, and the hours she spent with him each day in the basement made an enormous contribution to keeping him gentle. Animals have personalities they can be encouraged to develop or express, and Unity taught us just how diverse Christian's personality was.

We gave more time and affection to Christian than either of us had consciously given to anything or anybody else before. It was a commitment and a responsibility that gave our lives a sense of purpose we had not previously felt. Our days were spent with him, and at night we put him in his room in the basement, if we wanted to go out. One of us, quite often both of us at different hours, would let him out for a run around the shop late at night, before going to bed. As the shop was closed on Sundays, and Christian enjoyed any change of environment, we sometimes took him on outings. But there are not many places you can take a lion in London. One day we took him to Kensington Gardens. He was frightened by all the space, and although on a long lead he just hugged the fence for security. Not surprisingly, so many people gathered around him that further outings to parks were impossible.

We telephoned a Dr Barnardo's Home to see if the children would enjoy a visit from Christian. The woman we spoke to was rather surprised, but when we assured her that he was not 'dangerous', she accepted. We told her it was inadvisable for Christian to actually be with the children, and asked if there was an enclosed area for him. She suggested that the children could safely watch from inside the building, while 'the lion grazes on the grass outside'!

But Christian's visit met with an unexpected lack of interest. Little faces were pressed against the windows for a few minutes, and then the children returned to their toys. While we had afternoon tea with them, Christian was shut in a room. But a mischievous child let him out, and he came to look for us. The children screamed, scattered, and scrambled on to chairs and tables. Leaving chaos and probably many nightmares behind, we drove a confused little lion back to Sophistocat.

Christian was often invited to visit friends with us, and occasionally we took him. On one visit Christian pushed open a bathroom door, and we ran up when we heard a scream. It was difficult to know who was more frightened, Christian or our friend in the bath. The one household geared to incorporating a visit from a lion was that of Charles Bewick, Peter Bowen, and Margot the puma. We visited them quite often, and Christian spent Christmas Day there, while we went to friends in the country who had specifically not invited Christian. Margot was a beautiful animal with an attractive purr, but her behaviour was unpredictable, and it was difficult to relax in her company. She ended up living on an estate in the country. We had hoped, rather naively, that Margot and Christian would be friends, as we did not know any dogs strong enough to be his play-mates. But Margot was a different species, a different sex, and a year older, and she was intensely antagonistic towards him. He was just indifferent. In fairness to her, Christian was an intruder on her territory. It was pos-sible to have them in the same room together, but the only time he approached her Margot whipped her paw at him and scratched his velvety nose. Christian did not care, but he was to appear on television the next day!

In the middle of January 1970, a month after we had bought him, Thames Television heard that a lion was living at Sophistocat, and invited Christian to appear on *Magpie*, their children's magazine pro-gramme. He was only to feature for a few minutes so we thought he could cope with it. We drove out to the television studios at Teddington, rather excited but uncertain as to how Christian would behave. Unfortunately we had to have several rehearsals before the live performance, and we felt this was rather a pity, as Christian was less co-operative each time. He was confused and dazzled by the glaring studio lights, and frightened by the cameras when they advanced towards him. He was irritated at having to spend so much time on a lead, but long-suffering rather than angry. We regretted having accepted *Magpie*'s invitation, and nervously waited for the live performance. It was impossible to predict what Christian would do. One of us was to be interviewed, and at the same time try to keep Christian in camera range. He was apparently a great success, although what appeared to be a playful romp on the studio floor was in reality a struggle to stop him from running away.

Before his appearance on television, only a few newspapers had been interested in Christian. Suddenly he was widely known and there was much more curiosity about him, although the people who interviewed us seemed disappointed that owning a lion was less complicated than they had expected. The photographs they published were always of Christian yawning, with his teeth bared, and of course they looked like vicious snarls. The publicity was good for Sophistocat, but we realized that if it was to continue we had to have control over the printed pictures, so that Christian could at least be portrayed accurately. We met a photographer called Derek Cattani, who got on well with Christian, and a pictorial record of his life in London began. The newspapers were quite welcome to buy one of Derek's photographs if they wanted one.

People contacted us about wanting to use Christian in television commercials, or for various promotional purposes. He was such an expense for us that we were prepared to be mildly commercial, providing he suffered no stress or discomfort. He liked outings and enjoyed his few sporadic 'jobs', but in general he had a regular routine and a very stable life. He did a 'Nights on the Wild Side' photo shoot for *Vanity Fair*, advertising nightgowns. It was easy work, for he was just required to lie on a bed with a beautiful model and be photographed. The caption read:

Beware the man-hunting feline! Some stalk their prey in the jungle; others play pussy at home in lounging lingerie that clings and ripples with the same cat-like grace. Our lingerie isn't meant for lonesome evenings – put it on when you're planning to pounce, and if he doesn't, then get another cat for company!

Christian always enjoyed chewing hair, and the model had masses of it. He planned to pounce, and she became rather frightened, and was actually heard to say: 'My face is my fortune'! Restrained, Christian bit a hole in the goatskin bedspread and destroyed two satin pillows instead.

Several months later the airline BOAC (now British Airways) contacted us. They were opening a new route to Africa, and wanted Christian to make a very brief appearance at a promotional event, where he created quite a sensation and easily outshone the other African representatives: potted palm trees and avocados. He earned thirty guineas, which we paid into his account at the bank. Photographs of Christian opening this account appeared in the bank's in-house journal with the caption *Tough Customer at Chelsea*. It was an easy way of pacifying the manager about our overdrafts. We also did a series of Easter photographs for the newspapers, of Christian with six little chickens. He was amazingly gentle and there were no casualties.

When he was about seven months old and obviously leaving his cub days behind, there was suddenly a much greater and more widespread public interest. People were astounded that he was still so easy to manage. Experts, from London Zoo and the Feline Advisory Bureau for example, were astonished at how domesticated and well behaved Christian was. He was now regarded less as a novelty and more as a London personality owned 'by two Australians'. We were interviewed by several American and Australian newspapers and broadcasting services.

Jack de Manio, of the early morning *Today* programme on BBC radio, telephoned to invite Christian to be interviewed. At our suggestion he came into Sophistocat to meet Christian beforehand, and we warned him that Christian could be very inarticulate if he was not in the mood to converse, a disadvantage in a radio interview. As Christian had not yet roared, it was unlikely that Jack de Manio's listeners would be treated to his first attempt.

A car was sent to Sophistocat at 6.30 a.m. the next morning, and the three of us were taken to Broadcasting House. When we arrived the commissionaire blocked our entry to the building and, scarcely glancing at what was on the end of the lead, challenged: 'No dogs allowed in here – it's the regulations.'

'Do your regulations extend to lions?' we asked.

People do not argue with lions, and as we strode past him into the building he nimbly jumped aside.

Christian was far too interested in investigating the paraphernalia in the radio studio – such tempting cords and wires! – and looking at the faces pressed against the studio windows to even consider making any lion-like noises in his interview. We spoke briefly on his behalf, but the caption in the following day's *Daily Mail* read: *Mike-shy Christian flops on radio*.

We were mystified when we received a telephone

call from the BBC at Sophistocat later in the day. Without being offered any explanation, we were curtly asked Christian's value, but it was not a question we had ever had reason to consider. Several days later we read in Charles Greville's column in the *Daily Mail* what had happened. The headline was: *The Lion Behind Bars of Red Tape.*

> BBC regulations stated that animals brought into the building had to be insured, but because of some slip-up an hilarious situation built up with poker-faced officialdom going about the business of taking out a policy against damage to their departed guests. And, presumably, damage to the hosts, although as events had already shown by that time, the animal could hardly raise a yawn in the studio, let alone breakfast off de Manio and his team . . . and the value of the publicity-shy jungle king? £500 say the owners.

Newspapers invariably rang us if a lion or other wild animal attacked or killed someone anywhere in the world. We enjoyed disappointing them with glowing reports of Christian's impeccable behaviour. So many newspapers were inaccurate in their information about Christian that it was surprising we only received one hostile response. After an article had appeared in an American newspaper in April 1970, a woman wrote a long abusive letter. She concluded: 'What do you intend doing with him when you tire of him? He must now be growing up and after the life you have forced him to lead, he must be getting vicious and dangerous. No doubt you have had his claws and perhaps even his teeth removed, so I'm sure no zoo would want him. End his miserable life and have him put to sleep.' Declawing Christian had never been an option for us and, incorrect as she was about Christian's life with us at Sophistocat, we did share her concern for his future.

5

A Proposal

BY APRIL 1970, Christian was bored. He was then eight months old and rapidly outgrowing Sophistocat. Life had become repetitive and seemed to contain very few surprises for him. He was irritated that he had outgrown his favourite sitting spot on the stairs. It was too easy for him to climb all over the furniture in the shop, and at 130 pounds he was heavy enough to accidentally break the plate-glass windows. He was requiring more freedom, while we could only give him less. He was now capable of inflicting serious damage, and if he chose to behave badly we knew we could not control him. Whereas he had previously been an attraction for the shop, his size was beginning to frighten customers away. George Lazenby, the actor of 007 fame, came to visit with a friend of ours one afternoon. Christian was sitting in the window and even George could not be persuaded to enter the shop.

So Christian was spending most of his time in the basement, and increasingly resenting any form of restriction.

He was less contented and so were we. It had become an enormous strain on us. We had a responsibility towards Christian, but also had to avoid creating any dangerous situations. It was inadvisable to wait and see what form his frustrations might take.

The question of his future, which had hung over us from the very beginning, now inescapably confronted us. We revisited Longleat Safari Park which, as we had discovered before we bought Christian, seemed to offer the best living conditions for lions in England. This time we knew much more about lions. Because of the likelihood that Christian would soon be going there, we were proudly, but mistakenly, shown other sides of Longleat. We saw what an enormous commercial concern the Longleat–Chipperfield partnership had become, for, apart from the lions in the park, Mary Chipperfield provided an animal-hiring service for film and television companies. Also, some of the lions we saw were apparently part of a travelling circus. It was doubtful whether we could ensure that Christian would be introduced into a pride and live in the park, and not be used for more obvious commercial purposes. We decided that, for Christian, Longleat Safari Park was no longer a satisfactory solution.

To send him to a zoo would have been a betrayal of faith difficult for us to live with, but much more difficult for him. We now hoped to find someone with a large country estate who would love and care for him the same way that we did. Looking for other alternatives, we visited several private zoos. They were perhaps more rural than their city counterparts, but also more amateurish, and just as restricting and insensitive.

One afternoon the actor Bill Travers came into the shop, and was soon joined by his wife, actress Virginia McKenna. They had starred together in the 1966 film *Born Free*, the story of Elsa the lioness who had been returned to the wild by Joy and George Adamson. The film, like the book, had been a huge hit and although we were unfamiliar with either we recognised them. We assumed that their association with lions had brought them to Sophistocat. Disappointingly, they were only shopping for a pine desk, but we were unable to resist the opportunity of introducing them to Christian. They were astonished to see a lion run towards us and greet us affectionately. We talked about Christian's life with us, and they understood our dilemma about his future. They were pleased we had 'rescued' Christian from a cage at Harrods, but disapproved of the purchasing of and trafficking in exotic animals. Subsequent to starring in *Born Free* they had devoted their lives primarily to producing documentaries about animal conservation. Bill and Virginia had a much wider knowledge of lions than we had, and we asked them endless questions. We were flattered when they said they would like to come and see Christian again.

A few days later Bill came into Sophistocat with James Hill, the director of *Born Free*. We wondered why James had come, and why he questioned us so extensively about Christian. We were surprised and delighted, then, when Bill invited us to dinner at his house at Leith Hill near Dorking. He said he would like to show us a documentary he had made about lions that had begun their lives in captivity.

Dinner with film stars. It seemed fitting that James Hill should collect us from Sophistocat in his Rolls-Royce, and to the astonishment of the World's Enders we were grandly swept down to Surrey. After dinner we watched Bill's film *The Lions Are Free*, showing what had since happened to the lions involved in the filming of *Born Free*. Twenty-four lions had been used; yet, contrary to the theme of the film, only after a long struggle by Joy, George, Bill and Virginia was George allowed to rehabilitate three of them. None of the others would have the chance to live a natural life. In *The Lions Are Free* Bill visited the three lions George had successfully rehabilitated, and although they had not seen him for three years they remembered him, and he received a fond greeting.

The film ended with Virginia visiting Whipsnade Zoo to see Little Elsa, a lioness she had become particularly fond of during the filming of *Born Free*. Virginia called her name, and Little Elsa immediately recognized her, and ran to the bars of the compound. How could Virginia explain why they could not greet each other as they always had? The parallel with Christian was only too apparent, with the probability that within weeks we would have to condemn him to the same meaningless existence. Sensing our feelings, Bill smiled and said: 'I think we can help you solve the problem of Christian's future. We would like to arrange for him to be flown out to Africa, where George Adamson can return him to the wild.'

It was as if a prison sentence had suddenly, simply, been lifted. Of all the lions ever born in Europe, Christian had been offered an unprecedented reprieve. He was to go back where he belonged. Bill had contacted George Adamson in Kenya after his initial introduction to Christian at Sophistocat. George was extremely interested in the experiment of bringing a fifth generation European lion for rehabilitation in Africa, and was confident that it would be successful. Bill and James intended making a documentary for television which would help to cover the considerable expenses involved.

We did not have to be converted to Bill and Virginia's proposal. We did worry, however, in case

Christian had led such an unnatural life that we had de-lionized him to an extent that made rehabilitation impossible. George had assured Bill that Christian was still very young, and that many more generations of lions would have to exist in captivity before their natural instincts would be impaired. George intended to create a man-made pride of lions, incorporating Christian. We were to accompany Christian to Kenya, and help him start to adjust to his new life. George would live with the lions and feed them until they had established their territory, and were functioning effectively as a pride.

We realized it could not be assumed that Christian would have a long natural life. On average, lions live to eighteen or twenty years in zoos, but survive approximately nine to twelve years in the wild. They have to face territorial battles with one another, as well as droughts that decrease the numbers of their prey, and only the strongest survive. When lions hunt animals as large as buffaloes, if they do not kill efficiently they can easily be injured, or killed themselves. And Christian, with his Chelsea background, would be starting with disadvantages. However, he would escape a long, safe but totally pointless life in captivity, and would be given the opportunity to take his chance in his natural environment.

On our way back to London we spoke excitedly of the unpredictability of life. Where would Christian be now if someone else had bought him from Harrods? What would have happened if Bill and Virginia had not come into Sophistocat? By accident they had walked into our problem of Christian's future, and become involved in it. By buying Christian we had added new dimensions to our lives, and now unexpectedly to his. It would always have been an unforgettable experience for us, but one that could never have been remembered without regret if Christian were to live the rest of his life in captivity. George Adamson now offered the perfect solution to our dilemma over Christian, a lion it seemed who had been marked for an extraordinary destiny. When we arrived back in London that night, Christian fittingly made his first attempt at a roar. It was immature but recognizable, and we were immensely proud.

6

The Lion at World's End

BILL TRAVERS FLEW to Kenya to assist in negotiations which had already begun with the Kenyan government. He was confident that this unusual project would be acceptable, but the plans became more complicated than had been anticipated. In principle, permission to make the documentary was not a problem. It would be good publicity for Kenya and help attract more tourists, still the country's main source of revenue. Even if the basic motivation was to maintain this industry, there was also an increasing awareness among most African governments at the time of the need for the conservation and protection of animals. In the intervening years it has become obvious that even more urgent action is required, and there has been an alarming acceleration in the competition between man and wildlife for dwindling resources and habitats. The Kenyan government was also interested in having a record of George Adamson's methods of rehabilitating lions, and particularly the scientific documentation of such a unique experiment with a lion from England.

However, there had been considerable controversy in Kenya the previous year over the whole question of the rehabilitation of lions. A child had been slightly injured by one of George Adamson's animals, and this unfortunate incident provided an unfavourable background to our negotiations. Some members of the government viewed rehabilitation as a worthwhile project, but others felt that because of their earlier contact with humans such lions would be likely to approach people in the game parks, which could create a dangerous situation. Most people fear lions, and for Africans they are a traditional natural enemy or competitor, so why bring yet another potential man-eater from England?

But the Kenyan government finally agreed to give their permission for Christian to come to Kenya, if a suitable habitat could be found. The area would have to have water and game, and be in a region where there were no tourists, nor any immediate likelihood of tourism developing. It would have to be closed to hunting, and have no resident Africans or their cattle, which would be an easy kill for the lions. Bill looked at several possibilities while he was in Kenya, but had to return to England, leaving George to continue the search.

Meanwhile we had not heard from Bill or Virginia for several weeks. We did not dare telephone them in case we were told that it was no longer possible for Christian to go to Kenya. Finally Bill rang and explained the delay. He told us that George had just found two suitable areas, and it seemed likely that the Kenyan government would agree to the use of either.

Bill was confident enough to decide that filming would begin at Sophistocat the following Monday. The documentary, to be called *The Lion at World's End*, would be directed by James Hill, and was to start with a reconstruction of Bill and Virginia's first meeting with Christian, and then record the story exactly as it happened. The documentary would help to focus attention on the need for the protection and conservation of animals, and Christian, through extraordinary luck, was to be the subject and prime beneficiary of the film.

Our excitement was mixed with apprehension. After our experience at the television studios when Christian had appeared on the children's programme, we realized that it was impossible to predict how he would react to being filmed. We did not know to what extent we would be involved in the filming, although having no acting ambitions we could reject the old theatrical axiom 'Never compete with animals or children'.

Bill and James gave strict instructions that Sophistocat was to remain unchanged for the filming. We were asked not to cut our hair, and to be as flamboyantly dressed and as 'King's Road' as possible, instructions which we now rather regret. But as the shop would be closed to customers for one or two days, we thought it would be a nice gesture to the patient and tolerant owners if the shop appeared as smart as possible. On Sunday we repainted the walls and floor. It was a nicer gesture than we had intended, for it was an enormous shop and we worked hard all day. Christian was only allowed upstairs late in the afternoon, after the paint had dried on the floor. The last wall was still being completed when Christian knocked over the tin, splashing paint everywhere. Surprised, he jumped back, but slipped and fell. Scrambling to his paws, he then ran to the other end of the shop. We were dismayed; white paw marks covered the black floor, and Christian, required to appear as a lion for the cameras the following morning, was an unrecognizable white animal. Until very late that night one of us was repainting the floor while in the basement the other, armed with towels and turpentine, was struggling to clean Christian, who just thought it was a new game.

Next day Sophistocat was transformed into a film set. At first Christian was dazzled by the bright lights and confused by all the unfamiliar equipment and cameramen. However, this helped to keep him unusually subdued, and he only scattered the crew a few times. Bill and James were familiar with filming animals, and were very patient and undemanding. Christian, bored with the normal shop routine, enjoyed the day, and was so co-operative that Bill described him as a 'one-take lion'. It turned out that we were to participate fully in the filming, but we found we could forget about the cameras by concentrating rather intensely on Christian, who performed magnificently. Unfortunately our few lines of dialogue were later dubbed in excruciatingly broad Australian accents as our voices sounded 'too English'.

The following day we filmed at the Moravian Close, but Christian resented sharing his garden with so many other people and was very unco-operative. This was probably because of his strong territorial instinct, and although he loved chasing footballs, that day he totally ignored them. Bill and James wanted to film some slow-motion sequences, but when we finally succeeded in getting Christian to run or move, he stopped as soon as he heard the noisy slow-motion camera. Eventually, with no other alternative, we broke all our rules by encouraging him to chase us. We were irresistible and Christian could not believe his luck. Despite our torn clothing, the result was an enjoyable and worthwhile day's filming.

Several days later we saw the rushes of the first two days of filming. Christian looked beautiful, the slow-motion sequences of him running and playing were stunning, and none of us, not even Bill or Virginia, had seen a lion in slow motion before. For the first time we really appreciated his strength, power, and perfect co-ordination.

This might have been Christian's last visit to the garden, because the Moravian minister, although extremely fond of him, had reluctantly told us that he could no longer allow him to exercise there. He had been very tolerant, but other people had access to the garden, and could not now be expected to cope with Christian's boisterousness as we could. The day he had obstinately refused to get off the roof of the minister's car might also have been an influencing factor. But when we told the Reverend Williamson that we expected to be in Kenya in a few weeks' time, he kindly compromised by allowing us to come to the garden at 6.30 a.m. Our lives had to be considerably readjusted and Christian was now finding his life at Sophistocat increasingly monotonous and frustrating. He needed his day to be broken by an afternoon outing, so the early morning exercise did not suit him either. Bill and Virginia suggested building a compound for Christian in the garden at their house at Leith Hill, so that the three of us could live there until we left for Kenya.

When the compound was completed Christian left the King's Road and London for ever. Many of his World's End friends gathered to say goodbye. After living for several weeks fearing an accident, it was a relief to leave only pleasant memories behind. But we were also sad; our five very happy, unrepeatable months with Christian in London were over.

7

Country Life

BILL AND VIRGINIA'S HOUSE at Leith Hill was surrounded by an attractive, rambling garden, and although only thirty miles from London overlooked a valley of unspoiled countryside. When we arrived, their children and dogs were safely inside the house, and Christian had a taste of the freedom that awaited him in Africa. For the first time in his life he could do exactly what he wanted to do. He ran around the lawns, occasionally sniffing daffodils, and into the woods through the bluebells. It was a beautiful but incongruous setting for a lion. He continually came back to us, to show how happy he was.

It was necessary that Christian should live in the compound, but luckily he seemed very pleased with it. It measured twenty-five yards by fifteen, and enclosed a huge tree, several shrubs and a colourful gypsy caravan. He was so excited that his first reaction was to climb the tree, but as he had never climbed one before he was confused as to how to turn round and get down again. He just waited for us to help him. Bill thought that Christian would sleep under a shrub, but we suspected he would prefer to sleep in the caravan. We were to live in another caravan beside the compound. It was spring and the sun was shining and it was very peaceful in comparison with London.

That first night we sold Christian. A contract had been drawn up between us and the film company making *The Lion at World's End*. The whole project would be an expensive one, and while it was unlikely that we would not fully co-operate, we were required to relinquish to the company our ownership of Christian. We surrendered all legal control over his future. We were paid five hundred pounds, and we tried to view the transaction as a necessary formality in his best interests. But we felt guilty, and preferred to think of Christian becoming a Kenyan citizen rather than the mere property of a film company.

Christian slept in the caravan, of course. He greeted us effusively the next morning, relieved that we had not abandoned him and returned to London during the night. He seemed untroubled by his change of surroundings and oblivious of the fact that we no longer technically owned him.

We expected to be at Leith Hill only a few weeks, but George was still having difficulty in finding an area that both he and the Kenyan government found suitable, as the two he had originally proposed had not been approved. We were anxious to get Christian to Africa, but we dreaded to think how unattractive and desolate the district might be that finally met all the requirements. Always expecting to leave shortly, we waited while George continued searching, and the weeks passed. Fortunately the summer weather was usually pleasant. We spent restful days reading, sunbathing, and playing with Christian, and friends came down to visit. But as we were both basically city-orientated, one of us would occasionally go to London for a few days.

Unexpectedly, his time at Leith Hill became an important phase in Christian's life. He had fewer restrictions, a less complicated life, and a more clearly defined territory to live in. For the first time he experienced the natural cycle of a day. Sleeping in the caravan was a hangover from his life as a London lion. It was often hot and he was lethargic during the day, but he became rather boisterous in the late afternoons and evenings. After living at Sophistocat with Christian for five months, and regularly putting him to bed at about 8.30 p.m., we now appreciated that lions are naturally nocturnal. We spent most of our time in the compound, and he would look discontented if we were not with him. Yet he often ignored us once we were inside, for even if he did not want to play with us, as part of his 'pride', he just enjoyed the companionship. A double-gate system made entries and exits from the compound easy and safe.

Bill and Virginia had three young children and several dogs, and from his compound Christian watched their movements closely. He would have loved to be included in their games. At Sophistocat, if Christian had to be in the basement, he was unaware of what he was missing upstairs. He did not like being left out of anything and expected to have the freedom to decide if he wanted to participate. At Leith Hill a twelve-foot-high wire fence prevented him from join-ing in, but not from seeing the tempting games from which he was excluded. Unless we were with him, he paced the fence in frustration, and very quickly wore a path along it. By now it might have been a cage he was pacing in the same pointless way. After the initial mutual curiosity between Christian and the dogs, they quickly lost interest in one another. But if one of the dogs strayed too close to the fence, Christian would tensely crouch and flatten his ears, imagining he was invisible, but he forgot about his tail, which swished in excitement. Then he would charge the fence and succeed in frightening away the dog. This behaviour, and the number of times he succeeded in stalking and almost knocking us to the ground, meant that we felt George was right and his natural instincts had not been impaired.

We decided to begin Christian's preparation for Africa in a small way at Leith Hill. By comparisons we had made with other lions at Longleat Safari Park or in zoos, Christian was big for his age, but he needed to be as strong as possible for his new life. With constant exercise, and this outdoor life, he looked even healthier and continued to grow rapidly, his body now more in proportion with his head and paws. On a rope from his tree we hung a sack filled with straw and he adored attacking it, often swinging entirely off the ground. This was good practice for Kenya, and helped to develop his muscles. He had learnt to keep his claws sheathed when we were playing with him; sharp, inch-long claws are an important weapon for a lion, and attacking the sack strengthened them, and taught him how to use them efficiently. We also changed his diet. Lions in the wild usually kill in the evenings and have a varied diet. Christian was now given a small milk and Farex meal in the morning and one large evening meal. In addition to raw meat, he had dried meat, carrots and cow's liver, and sometimes we gave him the head or stomach of a cow. His presence at Leith Hill had not been publicized, and the local butcher, mystified by our meat orders, asked, 'What on earth are you two feeding, a crocodile?' As he knew we were living with Bill and Virginia, a lion would have been a far more reasonable assumption.

Christian's new diet improved his coat. It became thicker and softer, and was a beautiful lion-caramel colour. His partially black mane became more pronounced, and he was growing into an extremely handsome lion. He spent more time cleaning and grooming himself, although he was never as fastidious as most domestic cats. His tongue was so rough that his licks on our faces could almost draw blood. He had lost his milk teeth, and initiated his new ones by destroying several rungs of the ladder to his caravan.

He also had more scope to express himself at Leith Hill, and because we had more time to spend with him and appreciate him away from the demands of the city, our relationship with him grew even deeper and more affectionate. Unity came down from London several times each week to spend the day with him, and new games were invented. He particularly enjoyed playing 'wheelbarrows' with her, and became adept at tapping ankles and tripping people. He had a variety of toys, a new tyre, and several shrubs to play lions behind. He was content, and we found him irresistibly entertaining. Considering his size, he played extremely gently with us and remained easy to manage. It was perfectly safe for any of our visitors to come into the compound with him, except for children, who could accidentally be knocked over. A lion prepared to play 'wheelbarrows' must have, in addition to a sense of humour, a love for the human race.

Sometimes when it rained he grew quite wild, and then we stayed outside the compound. There was a difficult period when he became aware that he could easily prevent us from leaving by jumping up and holding us with his large front paws. Our smacks just made him more determined. Smacking a lion in a situation such as this required considerable audacity. But within a few days he realized that behaviour like that was self-defeating, for it meant we spent less time with him. He decided it was best to continue to co-operate.

We had bought Christian when he was very young, and it had taken months for us to build up our relationship with him. We admired the courage Bill and Virginia had shown playing their roles in *Born Free* and working with a cast of many adult lions. There was less opportunity for them to develop relationships similar to ours with Christian. As he was soon to leave for Africa, it was pointless for Bill and Virginia to become too friendly with him, but they often came down to his compound to see him. When they were with him, because of their experience with lions, they handled him well.

Christian's life at Leith Hill continued to be filmed, with particular emphasis on the beginnings of his re-habilitation. He had a strong fascination with the documentary's director James Hill, and most of our time was spent preventing Christian from jumping on him. James insisted that he was not frightened, but just did not want 'to have my new trousers torn'. He seemed to have new trousers on each day we filmed, and he directed more comfortably from outside the compound.

Bill decided to film Christian's first visit to an English beach. We were not enthusiastic; 3 a.m. is an unappealing time to begin a day, and we knew that it would be us Christian would trample on during the sixty miles there and back. He was now too big to travel in a car so we went in Bill and Virginia's Dormobile, a motorized caravan. It was the first English beach we had seen as well, and it was grey, dismal, and deserted. But there was a beautiful dawn, and we filmed several sequences of Christian and the four of us running along the beach. He had no intention of getting wet. He enjoyed the outing, but finally tired of waiting on the leash each time until the cameras were positioned. It was now unwise to irritate a lion of his size, so we took him home. His paw marks must have confused bathers later in the day.

Christian had now been at Leith Hill for ten weeks, and his life there was losing its attraction. And for us too; our caravan seemed to shrink in size daily. There had been days of incessant rain and we found the continuing delays depressing. Christian was becoming frustrated again, and the strain we had felt during his last weeks at Sophistocat returned. He occasionally climbed the wire of his compound and we added an overhang for security. We hoped that this was just a way of attracting our attention, rather than an attempt to escape.

On 12 August 1970, Christian celebrated his first

birthday. Unity made him a birthday cake of minced meat. There was one candle on top, and before Christian ate it and the cake, we made a wish that he would soon be in Kenya.

8

Christian's Parents

W<small>E HAD TO PREPARE</small> Christian for his journey to Kenya, as the long flight to Nairobi would be an ordeal. He was to fly with East African Airways, and regulations required him to travel by crate in the pressurized hold. It was an eleven-hour flight, but because Christian would be put in his crate at Leith Hill he faced at least fifteen hours' confinement. When Bill was making arrangements with the airline company, a representative said: 'There seems to be a mistake, Mr Travers. Surely you don't intend flying a lion from England to Africa? That's just taking coals to Newcastle.'

We investigated the whole question of Christian's flight very thoroughly, and telephoned several animal dealers and zoos for information about the best methods of safely transporting exotic animals. Our research revealed that there was no agreement or even any particular interest in the subject. We would like to believe that today animal transportation is a much more sensitive and sophisticated operation, but the sad truth is that while great care is taken with some animals, most are still transported around the world with little regard for their well-being. There is, for example, ongoing criticism of the conditions under which Australian sheep are shipped to the Middle East.

Some of the people we spoke to suggested a small crate to make it impossible for the animal to turn round; the less room, the less scope the animal would have to move and injure himself. We spoke to Oliver Graham-Jones, who had been senior vet at the London Zoo, and was well known at the time for the much publicized attempts to inseminate Chi-Chi the panda, who had to be transported from London to Moscow and back again. He advised that Christian should be mildly tranquillized by adding a sedative to his food, and that this would safely minimize any stress. Christian would probably sleep for most of the journey. We decided to order a crate large enough for him to sit upright and turn round in, with bars on one end and a sliding panel at the other. We specifically requested that there should be no rough surfaces or sharp edges on which he could injure himself.

When the crate was delivered we put it in his compound so that Christian would become familiar with it. He was fed in it, and we shut his caravan at night to encourage him to sleep in it. Each day we shut him into it for short periods so that the actual journey would be less of a shock.

East African Airways quoted a charge of two pounds per pound for flying Christian to Kenya, so we had to weigh him. We borrowed some scales from the even more mystified butcher, and tied them on to a rope hanging from the tree. We put an empty sack under Christian's stomach, lifted him up, and slipped both ends of the sack on to the hook at the bottom of the scales. He dangled helplessly but good-naturedly. It had been an effort for Bill and us to lift him, and we were not surprised when we saw that he weighed 160 pounds. A veterinary certificate of health was also required, and Christian was examined by a vet and inoculated with Catovac as some form of protection from diseases he would have no immunity against in Africa.

We had always wanted to see Christian's parents at Ilfracombe Zoo in Devon, and because of the long delay at Leith Hill we now had the opportunity to visit them. The zoo was typical of the many small country zoos scattered around England at the time, most of which have since closed. Ilfracombe is a popular holiday resort, and there were accommodation chalets attached to the zoo. There was a rather tacky fairground atmosphere, and depressingly small and basic cages for an assortment of chimpanzees, llamas, birds and even a few scruffy kangaroos. The lions were the star attraction, and Christian's parents Butch and Mary were the most magnificent lions we had ever seen. Despite their restricted living conditions, they looked very healthy. Unlike lions in the wild, which rest between kills until hungry again, Butch and Mary were fed daily so that they did not roar at night and disturb the holidaymakers in the nearby chalets. Christian looked very like his handsome, heavily maned, three-year-old father. They were an affectionate couple, but incessantly paced the cement floor of their small cage. The owner of the zoo was prepared to sell them for five hundred pounds, but we did not dare ask Bill if Butch and Mary could come to Kenya too.

We asked the owner about Christian's sisters and he told us the name of the animal dealer to whom he had sold them. We contacted this dealer, but as he had sold fifty-eight lion cubs in 1969 and kept no detailed records, he could only say that he thought they had been sold to a circus. Christian's sister at Harrods, who had been called Marta, had been purchased with a fraudulent cheque, and immediately resold to an undisclosed third party. The following letter sent to the Harrods buyer Roy Hazle provided some explanation:

> *HM Prison*
> *Jobb Avenue*
> *Brixton*
> *London SW2*

> *26th December 1969*

Dear Sir,
I have been told that you and the lady that works
with you have been worried about the lion cub I

*got from you. May I put your mind at rest and tell
you that it is now in a very nice home where it has
a very nice shed which is heated and a big garden
to play in. Two nice girls are looking after it as it is
the family pet and it gets the best of food to live
on. It has a dozen eggs and fresh milk every day
and plenty of meat, it's in the home of a film star.
So please don't worry about it and tell the lady
who used to look after it that it could not get a
better home. This will give her a little comfort
because I know she liked her very much. So please
don't worry it's being well looked after.*

    Yours sincerely,

    J. R. Styles

Despite this letter and further efforts to find Marta, no sign of her was ever discovered.

It seems ironic that while so many dogs and cats have pedigrees, it was almost impossible then to trace a lion's history, as so few records were kept. Today the situation has changed dramatically as virtually only major national zoos have survived, and to protect gene

Christian at Leith Hill aged ten months. His mane had begun to grow.

Opposite page: Virginia McKenna, Bill Travers, Ace and John, sitting on Christian's gypsy caravan at Leith Hill.

Above: Christian playing wheelbarrows with his best friend, Unity Bevis-Jones.

Above: John playing with Christian at Leith Hill.

Opposite page, top: John removing a twig from Christian's mouth.

Opposite page, bottom: John, Christian and Ace relaxing at Leith Hill.

Ace and John check on Christian in his crate at Heathrow Airport.

Opposite page, top: Loading Christian's crate onto the East African Airways flight to Nairobi.

Opposite page, bottom: George Adamson, Bill Travers, Ace and John with Christian at Nairobi Airport.

John, Ace and Christian at Kora.

pools it is necessary to keep precise records of individual animals. Butch had been purchased from the Rotterdam Zoo and may have been related to Elsa, because Joy and George Adamson had sent Elsa's sisters to Rotterdam from Kenya in 1956. Christian's family history was depressingly typical of the fate of animals in captivity, and by buying Christian we had unwittingly participated in its perpetuation.

Inevitably we compared Christian's future with the life of his parents. Freedom, instead of cement, bars, and boredom. Neither of us had visited a zoo where we believed that animals were both successfully and happily confined. Zoos should be constantly monitored, and certain standards maintained. However, we feel that being anti-zoo is unrealistic, since zoos today are doing invaluable scientific and genetic research which will ensure the conservation of endangered species. Zoos have to reinvent themselves and today are under intense scrutiny. Animals such as the Arabian oryx, the white rhinoceros in South Africa and the black rhinoceros in Kenya and Tanzania, which are almost extinct in their natural habitat, have been saved.

Christian had awakened in us a general feeling of responsibility towards all other animals. Bill and Virginia both said that their association with the lions during the filming of *Born Free* had had an enormous influence on their lives, and we frequently discussed with them the whole question of the conservation and protection of wild animals. We realized for the first time how drastically short-sighted man has been. Many of the issues we talked about have since become even more urgent, with increasing competition between man and wildlife for habitats and resources, including water, the degradation of the environment, and the ramifications of climate change. What has become even more obvious to us is the interrelationship between man and the natural environment, and how holistic any solutions will have to be.

Sitting in our caravan at Leith Hill we decided to create the best zoo in the world. Our zoo would be an example to all others, provide the best possible living conditions in captivity, and make accessible the most up-to-date information about animal life. World experts would work in conjunction with leading architects and designers to create an environment of the most sensitive and sophisticated nature. In addition to our perfectly exhibited, healthier and happier animals, we would provide lecture halls where zoologists and other specialists would lecture, and cinemas to show wildlife documentaries about animals in their natural state. We would have bookshops, and a library of books and films. Our zoo would become a centre of research and information, providing standards and advice on the conservation and care of animals in captivity for people all over the world.

We began to think how we could have designed a more sympathetic compound for Christian, one which would have resulted in his feeling less restricted. Why do so many animals in zoos have to live in compounds and cages which have such monotonous symmetry, no variety, practical but cold cement floors, and no evidence of any imagination in their design? Why not have compounds where humans walk through an enclosed corridor into the centre, and the animals have the freedom to walk almost entirely around the humans? There would be at least some transference of the feeling of restriction. Looking back, we are happy to note that some of these ideas have been incorporated into the redesigning and building of some enclosures, and that the animals' well-being has become a priority. Frankfurt Zoo in Germany has been a leader in this field, and at Taronga Conservation Society Australia some imaginative enclosures have been designed.

We waited for so long at Leith Hill that Christian outgrew his crate. We noticed that when he was shut in he sometimes pawed the vertical bars in frustration, and rubbed his pads quite raw. For his next, larger crate, we requested that the bars be placed horizontally, which would make it impossible for him to injure himself in this way. Although the company that made the crate had been supplying zoos and animal dealers for many years, they had never been asked to make this very obvious improvement. To us this seemed indicative of just how insensitive animal traders were.

After three months at Leith Hill, we were beginning to despair that George would ever find a suitable site for Christian's rehabilitation, and dreaded any alternative we might be forced to consider. We were depressed by the ongoing delay and the cramped living conditions. By now we were less star-struck, and we questioned how we were being portrayed in the film and feared that Christian was becoming just another animal in another Bill Travers and Virginia McKenna wildlife documentary. But Christian's story was unique. He was the undoubted star of the film and we were all bit players. And then, as it had in London, just when the situation seemed to be approaching breaking point, the next stage in Christian's life emerged just in time. A cable arrived from George Adamson. Christian would be leaving England for Kenya in a few days.

9

'Coals to Newcastle'

A T 3.30 P.M. ON 22 AUGUST 1970, Christian was led into his crate, not for the customary few minutes, but for at least fifteen hours. Pouring rain was to be his last memory of England. He was fed mild tranquillizers in pieces of meat, and then we carried his crate to the van which was to take him to Heathrow Airport. Lions have no luggage, and we could leave his leash behind as there would be no further use for it. Unity had of course come to Leith Hill to say goodbye to him, and tearfully promised to visit him in Kenya.

Following Bill and Virginia in their car, we travelled to the airport in the van with Christian, who was confused but not alarmed. The car containing our cameraman was stopped by the police for filming without a permit, for cutting across traffic and for causing an obstruction. But the combination of Virginia McKenna and a lion on his way to Africa persuaded the surprised policemen to be lenient, and the convoy was allowed to proceed. At Heathrow we drove straight out on to the tarmac and parked beside the East African Airways plane. Hessian was tied round the crate as insulation against the cold on the long night flight. The tranquillizers were proving effective, for Christian was quite relaxed, despite the noise from other aircraft and the curious crowd that gathered. At 5.30 p.m. Christian's crate was fork-lifted into the small pressurized hold of the plane. It was a dramatic and worrying moment, for we all realized there was a possibility that in the hold, alone amongst the luggage, Christian could die.

We left England at 7 p.m. with Bill and the film crew, and with Christian somewhere underneath us. The only scheduled stop, before Jomo Kenyatta Airport in Kenya, was in Paris one hour later. We were allowed to climb into the hold, where to our great relief we found Christian sleepy and calm. We decided that it was unnecessary to give him more tranquillizers, so we just slipped pieces of meat through the bars to him and refilled his water bowl. But the most demanding, longest part of the flight still lay ahead.

We landed in Nairobi at 7 a.m. Uninterrupted sunshine is assumed in Africa, as it is in Australia or California, but it was overcast and cold. While we had checked it was not the rainy season, we had overlooked the fact that it would be winter. On the tarmac we anxiously waited for Christian's crate to be unloaded. He had survived! His ordeal was nearly over, but no longer tranquillized he was very agitated. George Adamson was there to meet us, and he arranged for Christian to be wheeled off to an animal-holding compound, where he waited while we went through Immigration and Customs. Christian was relieved to be let out of his crate, and greeted us affectionately. George described him as 'a handsome, friendly little fellow'. Though he was uninjured and unmarked, Christian walked unsteadily and looked totally exhausted. His eyes were bleary, his coat had lost condition, and he seemed thinner. But we just could not believe that after all the delays and frustrations Christian was safely in Kenya, and had escaped the fate of a life of captivity in the United Kingdom.

At last we had met George Adamson, who had re-habilitated Elsa and knew more about lions than anyone else in the world, and was to introduce Christian into the wild. He was a surprisingly small and dapper figure wearing a stiffly laundered safari suit, and he had neatly trimmed grey hair and a pointed goatee beard. He was quietly spoken but had piercing blue eyes that seemed to examine us, and in his Foreword to this book he says he immediately had confidence in Christian but was not so sure about us! Only after a few days did he relax in our company. He was intelligent and amusing and admitted to his excitement and enthusiasm about the challenge of rehabilitating Christian.

The area allotted by the Kenyan government for this purpose was at Kora, near Garissa, 280 miles north-east of Nairobi. To reach Kora, a final track of twenty miles had been cleared through the bush by George's brother Terence Adamson, with an African labour force. Bill and George decided to make the journey in two stages, so as to provide sufficient time for the camp to be prepared for our arrival. It would also be easier for Christian.

Kora had been offered because no one else wanted it. George described it as a desolate, unattractive part of Kenya, where few Africans lived; there were disease-carrying tsetse flies, and in the wet season it could be inaccessible. The game, while not abundant, would be adequate for Christian and the other lions in the pride that George intended to form. For the exclusive use of this unwanted land the film company had to pay £750 a year.

Christian remained in the holding compound at the airport for two days. We stayed in Nairobi, and several times each day drove out to see and feed him. He was apparently content to sleep if we were not there, but the flight seemed to have exhausted and dis-orientated him. Our visits attracted enormous crowds of Africans and we realized that most of them had never seen a lion, or many other indigenous animals. Until the early 1970s, only tourists could afford to visit the game parks. Each time Christian walked towards the gate of the compound, the crowd stepped back apprehensively. When we talked to various officials at the airport, it was apparent that they did not see the point of trying to rehabilitate a lion, let alone flying one from England at such expense.

We visited Nairobi National Park and saw many animals in their natural environment, although we were only fifteen miles from Nairobi and the Hilton Hotel was clearly visible on the horizon. Bill had the opportunity to show George and several other people the rough cut of the English sequences in the film, and George was particularly interested to see a lion filmed in slow motion for the first time.

By the end of the second day Christian had fully recovered from his flight, so early next morning we left Nairobi in several Land-Rovers for the first stage of the journey. Christian travelled in the back of George's Land-Rover, and to our concern he paced relentlessly and quickly rubbed bare patches on his nose and fore-head on the wire barrier between him and the front seats. We stopped frequently to give him water and to try to pacify him, and George probably thought that we were unnecessarily worried about our pampered lion. On one of these breaks George warned us that Christian could run off if we let him out of the vehicle, and we were very proud when much to George's surprise he obediently jumped back in.

As the day progressed our surroundings became hotter, drier and more desolate. We had been depressed by George's description of Kora and now we could see for ourselves the nature of the country that Christian was to live in. We drove two hundred miles, and just before nightfall arrived at a temporary camp prepared by the safari company engaged to look after us, where we were to spend two nights. Christian was exhausted and we led him into a small compound that had been built for him. We decided to put our beds in with him, and he promptly climbed on to one of them and fell asleep. His first night in the African bush!

In the stillness and refreshing coolness of the African evening, we sat down to a superbly set table where Africans in flowing blue kaftans and red boleros and caps served us a delicious three-course meal. It was a surreal but pleasant surprise. At dinner George relaxed and asked us to call him George, and told us about the other lions that were to be rehabilitated with Christian. For his man-made pride George already had two other lions waiting at Naivasha. One was Katania, a four-month-old lioness who had been found and given to George, her mother being presumed dead. The other was Boy, a seven-year-old lion who had led an extraordinary life.

In 1963, when they were young cubs, Boy and his sister Girl were abandoned or lost and were found by Colour Sergeant Ryves of the Scots Guards regiment based near Nairobi. The cubs were lovingly raised by his wife Hildegarde and their two young daughters Jenny and Patricia, and were so friendly and popular that they became the regimental mascots. When the regiment returned to the UK there was even a suggestion that Boy and Girl would go with them, but luckily they were given to Joy and George Adamson for rehabilitation. Before being returned to the wild, the cubs were used in the film *Born Free*, and Girl played Elsa. Most of the other lions used in the filming were sold to zoos and circuses, which angered Joy, George, Bill and Virginia and created widespread controversy. In April 1965 Boy and Girl moved with George to Meru National Park.

Their rehabilitation had been successful, but in October 1969 Joy had quite by chance found Boy emaciated and badly injured, perhaps by a buffalo. He was operated on by the experienced wildlife vets Dr Tony Harthoorn and his wife Sue, and during the complicated procedure they inserted a steel pin into one of Boy's legs. Joy and George nursed him for nine months at Naivasha. It was a fortunate coincidence that Bill had contacted George about Christian at the time when Boy was almost well enough to be released again. George would leave our camp in a few days to collect Boy and Katania from Naivasha.

Next morning Christian had his first walk in Africa. We symbolically took off his collar, now to be permanently discarded, and followed him with Bill and George. The country was barren, only thorn bushes appearing to thrive, and totally featureless, and Christian, who had appeared so big in a London furniture shop, was dwarfed by his surroundings. It was extremely hot, and he just walked quietly, absorbing everything. Instinctively he knew how to remove thorns from his tender paws with his teeth, and we saw that the colour of his coat was a natural camouflage. He was obviously in his rightful environment.

Since it was a waterless region, we thought it unlikely that we would see any other animals, but late that afternoon a stray gombi, a large domestic African cow, came wandering towards the camp. Separated from its herd, it was looking for water or food. Christian saw the gombi, and immediately began to stalk it. The animal had enormous sharp horns, and George warned us to stop Christian, for he was so inexperienced he could easily be injured. He would not be restrained, so George raced to his Land-Rover and drove between Christian and the gombi, which then ran off. Before Christian could follow it, we both grabbed him to put him in the Land-Rover. For the second time in his life he snarled a terrifying warning, flattened his ears and we instantly released him. The gombi had disappeared and Christian, justifiably angry, reluctantly followed us back to camp.

George was impressed by Christian's perfect, instinctive stalking of the gombi, and explained to us how he had fanned out in a wide semicircle, using the natural cover of the bushes. He had been correctly positioned so that the wind would not carry his scent to the gombi and alert it. George said, 'We won't have any trouble adapting young Christian to the wild,' and again we felt enormous pride.

It was now eighty miles to our final camp at Kora. The road was rough and covered with powdery volcanic dust, and we had to drive very slowly. As we drew closer to the camp on the Tana River, to our relief the countryside became slightly more fertile and varied. Amongst other animals we saw elephant, waterbuck and some giraffe, and Africa began to come alive for us. We drove past a village whose inhabitants were wearing simple cloth wraps, necklaces and bracelets. They were the first Africans we had seen apparently living as they had for centuries, and not wearing drab Western clothes.

For the last twenty miles it was often necessary to use the four-wheel drive on the Land-Rovers, particularly when crossing sandy river beds, and it was obvious why the area was sometimes inaccessible in the wet season. We arrived late in the afternoon to find the camp in an unexpectedly beautiful setting. Our tents were amongst the distinctive doum palms beside the wide Tana River. Christian's long journey was over, and we could not believe we had actually got him to where he was to live. No doubt many challenges lay ahead, though, like meeting the other lions ... and simply surviving.

George left the next morning to collect the other lions from Naivasha, and was away for several days. We were thoroughly spoiled; our tents were comfortable and insect-free, our meals were provided, hot showers were prepared and our clothes were washed and somehow even ironed. Christian had a compound near the tents to sleep in at night. The Africans with the safari company were terrified of him, however, and if he teased them too often we had to keep him in the compound during the day as well. Because of the heat, we were all lethargic. Christian behaved like the worst tourist, avoiding the sun, and lolling on our camp beds at every opportunity, probably dreaming of cooler weather in England.

In the early mornings before it became too hot, or

in the late afternoons, we went for walks with Christian. We shall never forget the freedom of just walking with him, after the eight months in England so full of our imposed restrictions. He would bossily push his way in front of us, and always insist on leading. But he was easy to direct, and showed no inclination to wander off by himself. Fortunately on these walks we did not meet any other animals, for after our experience with the gombi we knew we would not be able to restrain him. If we went swimming, he sat in the shade and watched. He was fascinated by the baboons barking at him from across the river, and observed as well the hippopotami that occasionally surfaced, and the crocodiles that ominously slid into the water whenever we appeared.

Filming continued intermittently, and to everyone's surprise the 'King's Road Australians' adapted very easily to Africa compared to the English film crew. We were used to the heat and did not get sunburnt, could drive the vehicles and had a good sense of direction, loved the bush, swam in the river, and of course were to prove confident and at ease with lions.

In several ways Christian seemed very much a

beginner, with a lot to learn. With his big paws he was rather clumsy and inept at climbing rocks, and we often had to show him the way or help him. For the first time in his life he was not wholly dependent on us for amusement, but we were slightly concerned by his lack of interest in investigating anything on his own. We knew he was able to pull thorns out of the pads of his paws by himself, but he often just looked helpless and waited for us to do it. His pads were still soft, and because of the long walks and the thorns they became quite raw, but they quickly began to toughen.

He was content and free, and very gentle with us. Although now a large animal, he would still sometimes spontaneously leap into our arms, a gesture of affection that could now almost knock us to the ground. Soon other lions would arrive and we hoped they would make his life more complete.

10

A Lion's Lion

WHILE GEORGE WENT TO NAIVASHA to collect Boy and Katania, and we stayed by the river, Terence Adamson was building a permanent camp for George in much less attractive surroundings, several miles from the Tana River. This was to discourage the lions from swimming across the crocodile-infested water to the other side, which was a 'hunting block', where hunters pay for a licence to hunt specific animals, and there was a real danger that the lions could be shot. George intended to live at Kora for at least two years, which would give him time to form a pride, and the lions the chance to establish their territory and learn to operate independently. This second camp had several huts and tents within two large wire compounds.

A few days later George returned with Boy and Katania, and they were taken straight to his camp. In two days they had both recovered from their long journey, and it was time for Christian to be introduced to his first African lions. The initial test in his re-habilitation was that he should be able to assimilate into a life with other lions, and had not been disadvantaged by his life among humans. George explained that the introduction would have to be a gradual one, spread perhaps over weeks or months. He wanted to live with Christian in one compound, separated by a strong, high wire fence from Boy and Katania in the other. Living side by side, they would develop a familiarity, and eventually could be fully introduced. Compatibility cannot be assumed in any relationship, human or animal, but especially in this case with Christian and Boy, given their age difference and both being male.

Unsure of what would happen, excited but appre-hensive, we drove the unsuspecting Christian up to George's camp. He followed us into the first com-pound, and in the other one we saw Katania and Boy. Katania was tiny and cute, but our attention was riveted by Boy. He was enormous, impressive, and stood motionless with his eyes on Christian, who was instantly aware of his presence but unwilling to even look at him, understandably confused and frightened. We walked towards Bill and George, who were standing a few yards from the dividing wire fence. Christian was reluctant to follow, but slowly picked his way after us, his eyes averted from Boy. Bewildered, he crouched behind us, pressed against our legs. Katania sensed the impending events and wisely kept well away. Suddenly, with a deafening roar, Boy ferociously charged at Christian. Under his weight the wire gave slightly, and we all scattered. Poor Christian remained where he was, but cringed and snarled. Momentarily satisfied, Boy walked away. Christian was badly shaken and needed consoling. He leant on our legs and sat on our feet, insistent we did not leave him. It was obviously a shock for him to discover that he was not the only lion in the world, and, worse, that the first one he met was at least twice his size. We waited a few yards from the wire for about half an hour. Boy kept a nonchalant eye on Christian, who either sat on us, or hid behind our legs pretending to be asleep. Several more times Boy charged at Christian, who again cowered and snarled.

We moved away from the wire, the initial introduction over. Boy had behaved predictably, for as an adult lion he demanded submission from Christian, but George noted that Christian too had behaved predictably and correctly, cowering and deferring to an older male. Christian was very nervous all day, and although his eyes were constantly on Boy, he stayed close to us, well away from the wire. That night we put a bed for him between our beds, but our sleep was broken by Boy's powerful, haunting roars, which frightened both Christian and us.

Christian spent most of the next day on George's bed, although he was free to leave the compound if he wished. We were rather worried about him as he seemed too at home on the bed, and appeared to take no interest in Boy or Katania. He occasionally gave them a cool glance in the next compound. But late in the afternoon he walked to within a few yards of the dividing fence. Katania came over and really rather flirted with him. Christian was definitely interested but did not move any closer. Boy charged towards him and again Christian cowered. He then casually retreated and came back to us, and we felt that he had taken a positive step.

The following morning George constructed a small hatch between the two compounds so that Katania could be with either Boy or Christian. The crucial introduction would be between Boy and Christian, but Katania could be a helpful link. She tentatively came through the hatch twice, but Christian was of course asleep on a bed, and did not see her. Again we were concerned about Christian's lack of interest in communicating with the other lions. He pretended they did not exist, but we sensed he knew exactly what their movements were.

Later we took him for a walk, and he seemed relieved to be away from Boy and Katania. The countryside stretched endlessly, broken only occasionally by outcrops of rock. George had chosen the campsite for a variety of reasons, but Kora Rock, the large outcrop overlooking the camp, was ideal for the lions to use for observation. It was unattractive here in comparison with the Tana River, but still rather beautiful: various shades of grey and brown, and splashes of green around dried-up waterholes. Barren, and mainly covered by low, thick thorn bushes, it was a harsh area for the lions to live in. Christian had come to what could be described as another 'World's End'.

Back in the camp he teased the men constructing the huts; he bit a few bottoms and kneecaps, and jumped on whatever they happened to be carrying. These Africans adjusted to Christian but were always wary of him, as lions are their traditional enemies. George was interested to see that Christian, unlike most other lions, showed no colour prejudice. Boy, who would accept Europeans, growled fiercely each time an African came too close to his compound, but Christian did not share this dislike, and amused us all for the afternoon. He seemed a travesty of a lion.

In high spirits, Christian now became rather provocative with Boy. He focused his attention almost entirely on him, and a little later strode boldly up to the dividing wire and lay down. Boy charged and Christian turned and fled. But he went back a few minutes later and appeared to be teasing Boy, who was outraged by this impudence and again charged angrily. Christian even poked his head through Katania's hatch, but hastily withdrew it when Boy spotted him. Perhaps he had tired of having no contact with them, yet strangely he still seemed to feel it was more natural to be with humans than with lions. We certainly appeared to appreciate him more.

The next day George decided that it was time for Christian to meet Katania, who after her first exploratory ventures had been unwilling to leave Boy and come through the hatch to Christian. It was unusual for a fully grown lion and a four-month-old lioness to have such a strong, affectionate relationship, because in a natural pride the adult lion has little contact with the cubs. But since they had been living together at Naivasha, Boy, probably to his embarrassment, had been cast in the role of mother-substitute.

George led Boy out of his compound, and Christian, safely on the other side of the wire, stalked him as he walked past. Boy rushed at the fence, but his charges now seemed less convincing, and we suspected that he was rapidly becoming bored with this necessary display of authority. Interestingly, when he charged this time, Christian snarled as usual, but for the first time rolled over on his back, the gesture of submission from the younger lion that Boy demanded.

With Boy outside we could then take Christian through a gate into the other compound. He walked up to the other end, where Katania was pacing, distressed by her separation from Boy. Christian approached her confidently, and they exchanged a beautiful greeting, their heads gently touching. He was intrigued and continually licked and smelt her. Boy jealously watched all this from outside, but, after an initial charge at the fence to demonstrate his disapproval, he appeared resigned.

Christian and Katania played together, and although he was much bigger he was very gentle. She squealed on the few occasions he was too rough with her. He followed her, tapping her back legs and tripping her. This was a game that he and Unity had devised at Leith Hill. Christian was delighted to have a lion to play with, and afterwards we thought that he was rather smug and offhand with us!

Boy was led back into our compound, and Katania

ran through the hatch to greet him. After smelling her, he grimaced, baring his teeth to show his displeasure at Christian's scent, but another step had been taken. We were very uneasy about Boy's spending the night in our compound with us, as we had not been introduced to him either. To our horror he chose to sleep in our tent, and we did not dare argue. This really unnerved us. We did not know him and he did not know us. We were associated with Christian, who as a young male must have appeared as a threat to him. On several occasions he gently raised our arms up in his huge teeth and it was hard not to panic. Quick, unexpected movements can alarm and frighten lions, with dangerous consequences, and we tried to appear relaxed and not radiate fear. Boy urinated where he liked, staking out his territory, and we just tiptoed around him. We found him quite unknowable and privately felt he had had too many injuries, operations and anaesthetics for his behaviour to be predictable.

On the following day George thought that enough time had elapsed for Christian to be safely introduced to Boy outside the compound. It was a meeting we had all been waiting for, but we were aware that if there was a fight between them Christian had no chance. The decision was George's and we relied on his experience and judgement. We led Christian up on to Kora Rock behind the camp where George wanted them to meet. Then Bill and George led Boy and Katania up from a different direction. Boy and Katania lay down about fifteen yards from Christian, who was watching intently. For twenty minutes we stood nervously and watched and waited. Although impatient to make contact with Boy, Christian correctly sensed that it was not for him to make the first move.

Katania finally became bored with the tense situation and wandered towards Christian, and they greeted one another. Boy immediately stood up and charged at him. It was a very frightening moment, intensified by their roars and snarls. Christian rolled over on his back submissively, and, satisfied, Boy lay down a few yards from him. Although they had appeared to be fighting savagely, with paws and legs flailing, very little physical contact had been made, and Christian seemed to be unhurt.

After an interval of about ten minutes, Katania, who had wisely run off during the encounter between the other two, again came over to Christian, and triggered off another frightening performance. This time Boy walked away, leaving Christian badly shaken and looking miserable. He came over to us, and, comforting him, we walked with him back to camp, noting a few scratches and a slight limp.

Although it was an orchestrated situation, we had witnessed a natural introduction between an adult lion and a younger lion. If Christian had been any older, Boy would probably have killed him as a potential threat to his position. Despite our feelings for Christian, we felt we were intruding into animal society and protocol. Christian had instinctively known what his role was, and he had followed the conventions of the lion world by his submission. George commented that Christian had shown considerable courage by his determination to face Boy and not flee from him. Christian was obviously growing fond of Katania, but it was Boy's acceptance he was anxious to win. To gain this, he had to endure some ongoing unpleasant but necessary formalities.

We could now all live in the same compound. Over the next few days, Christian stayed as close to Boy as the older lion would permit. If Christian was too daring, Boy would charge, but the charges had lost their intensity. Christian concentrated adoringly on Boy, and even imitated his movements; he followed him around, sat down when he sat down, and lay in the same position. We often saw him lying just round a corner from Boy, a clever trick to get closer to him than would normally be allowed. He sometimes played with Katania, but she was a poor second to Boy. Christian was still affectionate towards us, but he was definitely a lion's lion.

Each morning we went out walking with George and the lions until they chose some shade in which to spend the hottest hours of the day. Christian followed behind Boy and Katania, but sat down and looked in another direction whenever Boy noticed him. In the afternoons we would find the three lions together, but Christian was always a few yards away, not yet an accepted member of the pride.

We had an extraordinary human/animal co-existence with the lions at Kora. It was a potentially very

Christian investigates the Tana River while John and Ace watch out for crocodiles.

The first camp beside the Tana River.

Three-month-old Katania with Boy, who had starred in the film *Born Free*.

Above: Christian meets Katania for the first time.

Opposite page: George Adamson and Christian at Kora.

A terrifying moment as Boy charges the wire, establishing his dominance over Christian.

Opposite page, bottom right: The dramatic first meeting of Boy and Christian outside the compound.

Opposite page, bottom left: Fortunately Christian reacted correctly and submissively and suffered only a few scratches.

Christian preferred to leap from rock to rock in
the Tana River, rather than get wet.

dangerous environment, totally reliant on George's experience and knowledge of lion behaviour. George's confidence in both lions and humans was sometimes questioned over the years by his detractors, but overall his faith had been justified. We spent ridiculous nights, often with the three lions in our tent. While Katania bit our toes or stole our blankets, Christian hid under a bed and Boy roared thunderously, following with any number of defiant grunts.

After a few days Boy greeted us in the same way he greeted George and his huge head would rub up against us. He had a seemingly placid nature, but a total assumption of superiority. As with all cats, everything had to be his idea, and he only did what he wanted to do. Filming had continued at Kora, and we often had to wait hours until Boy was suitably positioned. In contrast we just carried Christian to the required spot, or simply rolled him over to face the cameras. We found ourselves describing Boy as a 'marvellous' lion, and physically he was, but compared with Christian's youthful exuberance he seemed to have very little personality. Our praise of Boy was really just an expression of relief that he had eaten neither us nor Christian.

Christian had now been in Africa for several weeks. He was tougher than he had been and his pads had hardened, and he was growing into a very handsome lion. Bill described him as the 'Jean-Paul Belmondo of the lion world', referring to a French film star of the time. He had always been healthy, but one day he was suddenly listless. We thought he might be depressed by Boy's reluctance to fully accept him, but because of the whiteness of his gums, and his hot nose, George took his temperature and diagnosed tick fever. Christian had no immunity against the disease, but George, fortunately anticipating it, was able to inject him with the appropriate vaccine. He believed that Elsa had died from tick fever, and that if he had had this vaccine then, he might have saved her. Christian was very sick for two days, but after that he quickly recovered.

Now that Christian had been introduced to Boy, Bill and the film crew returned to England to edit the film. George suggested that we should also leave Kora for a short time, so that Christian could get used to life without us. We decided to visit other parts of Kenya and Tanzania, before returning to say goodbye.

11

Onward Christian

IN KENYA WE VISITED the Maasai Mara and in Tanzania the Serengeti, Lake Manyara and the Ngorongoro Crater. We saw a variety of animals such as wildebeest, zebra, antelope, herds of elephant, cheetah and leopard, and huge flocks of birds like flamingos, often in spectacular surroundings. We were most impressed by the dramatically beautiful Ngorongoro Crater, where we met some of the elegant Maasai people who have staunchly defended their right to a traditional lifestyle with their cattle, even more threatened today than it was then by the competition for land and resources. It was there that we saw our first lions in the wild: three cubs and two lionesses. While tourism is an important industry and gives employment to many Africans, there was something disturbing about 'wild' lions that appeared unconcerned by the Land-Rovers encircling them, and the tourists leaning out of the windows taking photographs. One woman in a game reserve who had been driven by a guide to see the unusual sight of a lion guarding his freshly killed buffalo from vultures said, 'I've come to see kills, not carcasses. Drive on.'

Conditions in the lodges where we stayed varied from nights under canvas to the luxurious. All the lodges were expensive, and full of enthusiastic middle-aged tourists, who seemed to feel that the cost of their African holiday was justified if they saw one lion. While these tourists were obviously loving their African experience and expanding their awareness of animals in the wild, having flown with our own lion to Africa we were less easily satisfied. We had been spoiled by our weeks at Kora, living with several lions, and at a pace at which it was possible to absorb a deep feeling for Africa. Rather than have many animals paraded before us, we preferred to see a few of them unexpectedly, or to sit quietly by the Tana River for hours watching the shy waterbuck, baboons, oryx and elephant come warily for their evening drink.

We decided to visit Joy Adamson at her house Elsamere on the shores of Lake Naivasha, a drive of one and a half hours from Nairobi. Prior to relocating to Kora, George had been staying there monitoring Boy's recovery from his injuries and operations.

Joy Adamson was born in Austria and first went to Africa in 1936. She was a very talented woman with great enthusiasms, often allied to her partners' occupations. She was a very fine botanical artist (her second husband Peter Bally was a botanist), and also painted animals, birds, and a definitive series on the tribes of Kenya. Many of her paintings are in the Nairobi Museum. Joy and George met in 1942 and had a volatile marriage and relationship which lasted until her death.

After Elsa the lion cub was raised and rehabilitated by them, their lives were devoted to the conservation of animals and returning different species to the wild. From George's diaries Joy wrote *Born Free,* which was published in 1960 and followed by a film version in 1966. Both were huge worldwide hits.

In 1961, Joy set up the Elsa Wild Animal Appeal, now called the Elsa Conservation Trust. The documentary about Christian's rehabilitation and the allotment of Kora for this purpose gave George financial independence from Joy for the first time, and a place to live with his lions. Joy resented this, so it was with some trepidation that we drove up to Elsamere, where to our surprise the sofas were upholstered in lionskin. When we dared ask her about it, she brushed our concerns aside with, 'There are good lions and bad lions.'

Despite her reputation for being difficult and frequently falling out with people, we found her reasonably friendly. She was intelligent and interesting, and curious about Christian's background. She was relieved to hear that Boy was recovering from his injuries, although he was still limping. She was sceptical about Christian's chances of surviving in the wild. 'Your stupid fat English lion will be killed, and so will George,' she said. Joy was very keen to visit Kora, but was annoyed at being excluded from the work there. Despite the huge earnings from *Born Free*, she never financially supported George's work. When she did visit Kora she was very anxious to be photographed with Christian, but subsequently declared, 'It is time for humans to leave the lions alone.' This was the conundrum of the Adamsons' lives: the very success of their work, facilitating the independence and self-sufficiency of the animals, made them redundant.

Like some other people who love animals, she did not see the irony in her often disastrous human relationships or her reputation for harshness with her African staff. She was murdered by one of them in 1980 after a dispute about pay.

On our way through Nairobi, we took a sample of Christian's blood to the vets Tony and Sue Harthoorn. George had correctly diagnosed tick fever, and they told us that there was a slight chance that it would recur. It was fortunate that George had the vaccine to combat it. Boy and Katania were also susceptible to the disease, just because they had moved from one part of Kenya to another.

On the long drive back we lost our way in the darkness, and were alarmed when our Land-Rover was flagged down by what looked like almost naked, spear-holding warriors. We thought we should stop, but quickly wound up the windows. We were embarrassed to see they were friendly young African children with sticks, merely wanting cigarettes. In English, they directed us to Kora and 'Kampi ya Simba where the white man keeps lions'!

We arrived at George's camp late that night. He was concerned about Christian, who for the first time had not returned with Boy and Katania in the evening. George had looked for him and called him, but he had not appeared.

Within a few minutes of our arrival, however, Christian came running towards the camp. We had been away for a fortnight and, wildly excited, he leapt all over us. George believed he must have had a premonition we were returning; he thought lions have a sixth sense that humans have either lost, or never had. On visits to his other lions after their release in the wild he often arrived in a deserted camp, only to be mysteriously joined by the animals a few minutes later.

Christian had obviously missed us and gave continuous happy grunts while leaping on us and licking our faces. When we sat down, he would clamber on to one of our laps, then stretch across to have at least part of his body, his front paws, on the other one. He excitedly jumped on the table, creating chaos and making eating impossible, and we were not allowed to sleep.

We were delighted to see he looked so well, and that George was growing fond of him, and found him as amusing as we did. One night he had unwisely made him a snack of powdered milk, a great favourite from his English days. And now, every night, Christian followed George around, tapping his ankles and butting him with his head, until he relented and gave him his powdered milk.

Disappointingly, Boy had still not totally accepted Christian, although there had been an improvement. George thought Christian sometimes seemed depressed by his unrequited adoration of Boy. He and Katania were now very friendly, and George thought that now it might be Boy's jealousy that was prolonging the ongoing tension.

He told us of an incident which had happened the day we left Kora. He had followed the lions on their morning walk, and quite close to the camp he had seen an enormous rhinoceros. Boy and Katania tactfully moved well away from it, but to George's alarm Christian began to walk towards it. He stalked it perfectly, and had come to within a few yards when the rhinoceros suddenly turned and saw him and, snorting with rage at Christian's impudence, charged. Christian sprang eight feet in the air, over a bush, and fled. George was very amused, but hoped Christian had learnt his lesson.

Already Boy had spent several nights away in an attempt to establish a territory. He chose the opposite direction from a wild lion heard roaring on several occasions. However, it was impossible for a single fully grown lion to establish a territory alone and George told us he planned to bring two lionesses up to the camp. He had been offered these lionesses of about Christian's age, which had been captured after they had frequently attacked domestic cattle and without George's intervention would have been killed.

This time we spent only a few days with George and Christian. Each morning we walked with the lions until they chose a tree or bush where they could shelter from the sun. Christian always accompanied Boy and Katania, but Boy suffered his presence rather than encouraged it. In the afternoons we walked with George to find them, fascinated by the way he could identify and follow their spoor (paw marks), and his deep knowledge of wildlife and bushcraft. The lions returned in the evenings to be fed, and George sometimes had to drive many miles to a hunting block to shoot waterbuck or other game for them to eat. He hoped they would soon be self-sufficient.

We loved talking to George and had long conversations with him, not only about lions, but also about Australia and our lives in London, and his life. George had been born in 1906 in India, where his father was in the British army, and he was educated in England. He had spent most of his life as a game warden with the Department of Wildlife in Kenya. Although he had led an isolated life, he kept in touch with events in the outside world. He had returned to England only once since leaving school, and he was interested to hear how London had changed so many years later. He was kept informed by visitors, friends and admirers around the world, and *Playboy* magazine which he read 'for the interviews'.

He talked of his early days as a hunter, and how, when he first realized the threat of extinction that faced so many animals, he had become increasingly concerned for their conservation. Since Elsa's death he had devoted his life to rehabilitating lions.

George loved lions passionately, and believed it is possible to attain an understanding and communication with them that is unusual if not impossible with other animals. He admired their dignity and immense capacity for love and trust and he wanted to continue living at Kampi ya Simba until the lions were no longer dependent on him. He felt Boy was about to grant Christian the acceptance he longed for, and that the other lions would complete the nucleus of a pride that would include Christian. He was confident that all the lions would be successfully rehabilitated.

Through a series of extraordinary coincidences we had delivered Christian to Africa and to the world's most knowledgeable and sympathetic lion expert. Christian now had the freedom to take his chance in the wild. We could not have imagined or dreamed of a better outcome, and this tempered our sadness at leaving him. Life would initially be very empty without him, and tears were shed. We wondered if we would ever see him again, but Christian, after a journey of several generations and thousands of miles, had returned to where he belonged.

12

Christian's Progress

SEVERAL MONTHS AFTER WE LEFT Kora and returned
to London we had news of Christian, Boy, and
Katania in a letter from George, part of which
follows:

> I expect you have heard about the tragedy of
> poor little Katania. One evening last month the
> three lions pushed off towards the river after
> having a good feed of meat. They did not return
> the following morning, which was nothing
> unusual, as on several occasions they had been
> absent for two or three days, once even for five
> days. I went searching for them two days later
> but without success. In the early hours of the
> next day Christian appeared alone. This was a
> little worrying as usually he and Katania kept
> together, while Boy went off looking for girls.

However, I thought Katania must surely be with Boy. Early next morning Boy arrived, alone.

Now there was real cause for alarm, and Christian seemed just as worried as I was. I started an intensive search on foot and by Land-Rover. I took Christian walking with me, relying on his powers of scent for help. It was not until four days later that I found the spoor of the three lions on the bank of the river, about three miles below where you stayed by the Tana before moving up to my camp. It was plain to see that Christian and Katania had been playing, racing up and down along the bank. I crossed to the far bank but found Boy's tracks only. On the near side, there were only the tracks of Christian leaving the river, I think Katania must have tried to follow Boy into the water, but being so much lighter and smaller, was carried down by the current, and before she could make the bank, she was taken by a crocodile. Even at her age lions are very good swimmers and it is unlikely that she would have drowned. It is a sad loss which I feel keenly, as do Boy and Christian. The joy has gone out of them.

About a fortnight ago, Boy went off on another foray across the river and returned with a girlfriend. I could hear them around the camp for three days and nights. One night while Boy was busy with his lioness, I heard Christian growling near the edge of the bush in front of the camp. By the light of a torch, I saw him facing another wild lioness of about his own age.

Boy and Christian are now good friends. In fact, Boy often takes the initiative in the greeting ritual of mutual head rubbing. Christian has started to accompany Boy in his roaring! A trifle immature, but a darned good effort. His voice promises to be even deeper than Boy's. A few days ago, there is reason to think that the two met up with the lionesses again, who may have made a kill, as both returned looking well fed and not in the least hungry after three days.

I soon hope to collect the lionesses that you know about. From the description given to me, I would say they are about fourteen months old, which means that they should have already had experience of hunting with their mother. They should be a big asset, provided I can gain their trust and friendship.

George Adamson
12 January 1971
Kampi ya Simba, Kora

Bill Travers flew out to Kenya shortly after we received this news from George, and wrote to us on his return to England:

Dear John and Ace,
I arrived back from Africa at the week-end. I can imagine your concern over the past weeks and thirst for news of Christian, so before I go into details of how he is making out, let me tell you first of all that he is both alive and well. He does

not seem to have had a day's sickness since the tick
fever he had when you were both out there. And
he is very much alive I can assure you – my paw-
marked khaki trousers will bear witness to that.
He is a good deal heavier too, well over 200 lbs I
would say at a guess, though sometimes when he
greeted me fondly it felt considerably more. I am
quite sure we could never now lift and suspend
him from the local butcher's scales as we once did
in England to find out his exact weight for the
flight to Kenya, even if he would still allow it. He
is as high at the shoulder as any fully grown lion,
even as tall as Boy who, as you know, is a big
lion. But in spite of his size he is as affectionate
as ever. He gives George long ceremonial greetings
with his head, licks him with his sandpaper
tongue the moment George puts a foot outside
the wire fencing that runs round the camp,
inside which Christian is now no longer
allowed.

However, this affection does not seem to be
hampering the progress of rehabilitation, but in a

strange way gives George the control that he will continue to need during the months that it takes to establish the lions first as a family and then as guardians of their territory.

By the way, I noticed that his coat seems to have adjusted to the hotter climate and is thinner, much finer and smoother, which makes him look more streamlined, more mature and certainly emphasises his now fine athletic figure. He is really quite a magnificent lion, and it would be hard to find anything to criticise in his appearance, except perhaps his feet. They are still enormous. I can only think if he grows big enough to make them look normal he will be, without doubt, the biggest lion in Africa.

After you left Boy and Christian became the greatest of friends – in fact quite inseparable, and the little cub Katania, who as you saw adored them both, found herself as they flopped over each other, the protesting centre of a sandwich.

Unfortunately, this friendship, as you have already been told, was short-lived. I won't therefore dwell on the circumstances which led us to assume the death of Katania, except to say it was doubly tragic. Not only had Boy and Christian lost their little friend, we'd also lost the only female in George's pride.

However, there is good news too, to compensate. The two lionesses George has collected are about the right age for Christian – a few months younger than he is. Unlike Christian they are already quite wild, and though too young to kill must have learned from their parents how to hunt. They must also have some knowledge of the strict rules of lion society. I think Christian will benefit greatly from his association with them as the pavements of Chelsea and the soft country life at our home were hardly the best schooling for the life he is now starting to lead. George, of course, is delighted as it is essential to have at least one female in the family or pride which

*we hope eventually will be able, with George's
help, to establish itself in the Tana River area
and enjoy freedom and a natural expression
of life.*

*Well, I am sure there can hardly be a day that
you do not talk or at least think about Christian,
George and Boy. I can only tell you that the last
picture I took with me, as I drove away from
George's camp, was one of the three friends
standing happily together for a final word outside
the gate of their 'home'. A pat, a handshake,
and they remained watching my Land-Rover
as it started bumping down the long trail back
to Nairobi and civilisation. I looked back as
often as I dared take my eyes off the road and
saw Christian rub against George, who fondled
his slight mane, then wander off to Boy, to
greet, nudge and no doubt provoke him into
starting some wonderful sprawling lion
game.*

*I felt strangely happy. I think if it were not
for George Adamson and for people such as*

*yourselves, Christian would have ended up in very
different circumstances...*

   All the best,
      Yours,
         Bill

13

The YouTube Reunion 1971

AFTER BOY AND Christian's first dramatic encounters and prolonged standoff they finally became inseparable, particularly after the death of Katania. In his 1985 autobiography *My Pride and Joy*, George Adamson described the early days at Kora with Boy and Christian as 'some of the most enjoyable of my life'. The wild lions, however, resented the intrusion into their territory of Boy, Christian, and the two lionesses Monalisa and Juma who had arrived from Maralal, in northeastern Kenya. As the only mature lion and head of the pride, Boy had frequent confrontations with these wild lions. One day he returned to camp with deep wounds on his back, and George treated them in the safety of the compound. The wild lions waited expectantly outside and, unable to get at Boy, attacked and killed Monalisa.

Boy seemed to be in great pain from this latest

injury and now wandered off more frequently on his own. However, Juma and Christian, who had become good friends, were left unprotected. George was becoming increasingly concerned about Boy's well-being.

George was then given two eighteen-month-old lionesses from the Nairobi Park Orphanage, whom he named Mona and Lisa (in memory of Monalisa), and a boisterous young male called Supercub. George's plans to create a self-sufficient pride were progressing, with Christian an integral part of it.

But George's plans and Christian's rehabilitation suffered a tragic setback. On 6 June 1971 Boy had been away for a few days and the other lions were on Kora Rock behind the camp. George realized Boy had returned when he heard him drinking from the water trough outside the camp compound. Suddenly George heard cries from the same direction, and grabbing his gun ran out to see his African assistant Stanley in Boy's jaws. George shouted at Boy, who dropped Stanley. George shot Boy dead and he rushed to Stanley's aid, but the assistant died almost immediately.

George was devastated. Stanley had been instructed not to go outside the compound, but he had ignored George's orders and now he had lost his life. George also mourned one of his favourite lions, whose life had been intertwined with his ever since Boy was a cub. The 'accident', as it came to be called, made international news and was fully investigated by the local police and the Game Department. George's work was criticized for endangering lives, and the future of the whole project was temporarily put at risk. However, George had many supporters, including government ministers who appreciated the value of the Adamson name to Kenyan tourism, and he was allowed to remain at Kora.

We had been living in London writing *A Lion Called Christian*, which was due for publication in November 1971. We had intended to fly to Kenya and visit Christian with a film crew, as they had nearly completed the second documentary *Christian the Lion* and wanted to include a reunion sequence, but when we heard George's shocking news we delayed the visit for a few weeks.

When we arrived in Nairobi we were told by

various people that there were rumours that Boy had always been the least predictable of the Adamson lions, and that Stanley had been 'disrespectful' and careless around Boy on several occasions.

We flew on from Nairobi, and when we landed on the earth strip Terence Adamson had cleared a few miles from the camp at Kora, George was waiting to meet us. He was looking well, considering the tragedy, and we hoped our visit would be a diversion for him. We tried not to bombard him with questions about Christian as we drove back to Kampi ya Simba. Although George had not seen the lions for a while, they had appeared that morning and were now resting from the heat in the shade. We waited anxiously in the now much more comfortable and permanent camp. We could only guess at the reception we would get from Christian, but we felt deep inside that it could only be a loving one, and that he could not have forgotten us. Could a year apart have changed our relationship?

Ace described the reunion in a letter written to his parents at the time:

*The lions were 'lying up' about half a mile away,
and we had to impatiently wait several hours
until it was less hot and the lions would be likely
to move. Finally, with the film crew, we walked in
the direction of the lions, and waited at the base of
Kora Rock while George went over the top to call
Christian. Shortly afterwards Christian appeared
at the top – about 75 yards away from us. He
stared hard at us for a few seconds, and then
slowly moved closer for a good look. He stared
intently. He looked marvellous, and up on the
rocks, he didn't appear much bigger. We couldn't
wait any longer and called him. He immediately
started to run down towards us. Grunting with
excitement, this ENORMOUS lion jumped all
over us, but he was very gentle. Soon we had 3
lionesses milling around us – about Christian's age
but not nearly as big. And Supercub, a delightful
5 month old male. Quite unforgettable of course.
Christian showed his affection in exactly the same
way, had all his old tricks & some new ones.
George is just captivated by him – as everyone is.*

He is the best natured lion George has seen – with humans and lions. He is in superb condition – much sleeker, and because of the heat his mane hasn't grown much. His spots have finally faded more. His front teeth are a frightening 1½ inches of white ivory! It was difficult to adjust to his size – he was about 160 lbs 10 months ago, now George thinks he is about 300 lbs. We gave him enormous respect, and were a little less frivolous with him – a much more mature lion, but still most entertaining. Undoubtedly head of the pride – he rather enjoyed playing out the role for us. George is delighted with their progress – they have become a 'tight unit', and apparently they could begin to kill quite soon, which sounds bloody, but will be essential for their survival.

Nairobi 20/7/71

Reading these words again so many years later, like looking at the reunion footage, brings back so many memories of what was undoubtedly one of the most extraordinary days of our lives. Although it was nearly

Christian picks his way carefully through the thick thorn bushes at Kora.

Above: George, Ace, Christian and John rest in the shade at George's camp.

Opposite page: Christian's first night in the African bush, and a reassuring paw on John's face.

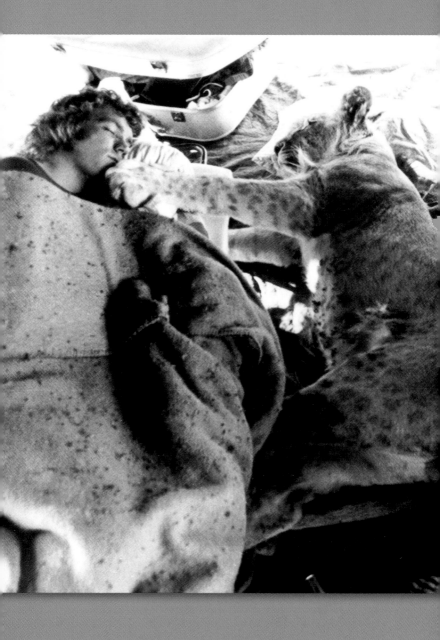

THE REUNION IN 1971.

Main image: When he recognizes Ace and John, Christian runs towards them.

Top images: Christian jumps up to greet Ace and John.

The lion had doubled in size in the year since Ace and John had seen him.

In 1972 Ace and John returned to see Christian.

Again he had doubled in size but still remembered them and greeted them with the same affection.

Below: Ace and John with Christian on the rock overlooking George's camp.

Christian surveys his kingdom at Kora.

a year later, George had had complete confidence that Christian would remember us, and that we would be safe. We instinctively felt this too. We know people expect us to have been frightened, but we had no fear of him. We knew Christian so well and could read his behaviour, and had built up such trust with him, but could this have changed? We were so excited at the thought of seeing him, but there was also some anxiety as no one could really predict what would actually happen. Any doubts dissolved as Christian – once he had ascertained that it was us and we called his name – ran towards us with such enthusiasm and affection, making his excited little grunts and with a loving expression we recognized. As this now much bigger and even more handsome lion ran towards us, our only concern was whether we could physically handle the joyous leaping up on us and hugs we now knew were inevitable. He was surprisingly gentle with us under the circumstances, and we were all surprised at how exuberant this welcome was, and we were just ecstatic. We weren't even frightened of the other lions who had materialized and were now milling around our legs, and although Mona, Lisa, Juma and Supercub had had very little human contact, the atmosphere was so infectious that they too were caught up in it.

We were woken by Christian's roars each morning and they were impressive for a two-year-old. We spent the next few days enjoying George's normal camp routine, walking with the lions in the morning, sometimes sitting with Christian in the shade while they dozed, or setting out with George in the late afternoon to find them. Now, a few weeks after the death of Boy, Christian was relishing his position as head of the pride. We let Christian totally dictate our relationship with him. If he wanted to play we played, and if he wanted to be affectionate we reciprocated. At other times we were superfluous to his life, or a distraction, and we just left him alone.

It was fun and challenging getting to know the other lions, who were virtually wild and had all arrived at Kora very wary of humans. Looking back now at this lion/human interaction, we wonder if George possibly had too much confidence in all of us. One day Christian was leading us on a walk when he suddenly charged off into the bush with a huge growl, chasing after Mona and Lisa. They had been crouched waiting in ambush for us, probably for fun, but it could have been a very dangerous encounter if we had reacted with fear or been knocked over. We were very touched by Christian's protective attitude. Supercub had a cheeky extrovert personality and Lisa was a very playful lioness, but Juma and Mona were both very shy. In a letter to Sir William Collins, George wrote that ironically Christian, the lion from London that had had the most contact with humans, was the easiest lion to rehabilitate at Kora so far.

Kampi ya Simba was now much more established. George's brother Terence had built a number of permanent huts, the walls ingeniously constructed of chicken wire covered with hessian and then painted with numerous coats of cement and topped with palm-leaf roofs. The largest of these simple but effective buildings was the mess hut, which was the hub of the camp where George kept the radio telephone, his only link with the outside world. He also had an ancient typewriter, and a jumble of books, letters, diaries and photographs.

There was now a generator to power the freezers, which were mostly stacked with camel meat for the lions, purchased from the nearest village Asako, forty miles away. George's cook Hamisi cooked for us on an open fire in his own lion-proof compound.

The menagerie surrounding the camp included noisy guineafowl, ravens, friendly hornbills, monitor lizards, the occasional unwelcome snakes and scorpions, and the ever-waiting vultures that Christian was always chasing away from his old bones.

While it was a unique experience to visit Kampi ya Simba, we only planned to stay a few days, as the less contact the lions had with humans the better. Visitors to the camp were often disappointed when George would not allow them to approach his lions, so we were very privileged. The lions had to be self-sufficient, and were encouraged to be wary of humans, yet we had been welcomed by Christian in the most wonderful, loving, unforgettable way. That day was a euphoric experience for all of us, lions and people. Now via YouTube nearly forty years later, that experience has been shared by millions of people all over the world.

We were obviously sad to leave Christian, but he was clearly contented, and everything seemed to be going well. The wild lions had been quiet for a while, and there was a calmness at Kora. When we left and our small plane circled the camp, Christian and the other lions looked up from Kora Rock, and as one of us waved back to George in the compound the other shed a few quiet tears. In this unpredictable and often hostile environment, would Christian's good fortune continue?

14

The Final Farewell 1972

IN LONDON WE were kept informed of any news, and
in January 1972 we received two letters from Kora.
George wrote:

> *I have been very lucky in finding a young man to*
> *help me. Tony Fitzjohn, aged about 27. A bit of a*
> *wanderer who has tried his hand at many*
> *occupations. Very fit and capable.*

Tony, it seemed, had originally written to Joy
Adamson asking for a job, but she had suggested he
work for George, who she felt needed an enthusiastic
and multi-skilled young helper. Tony too wrote to
us:

> *Dear Ace and John,*
> *Although we've never met I thought I'd put a*

*few lines down. I've been helping George for some
time and have become as fond of Christian as you
must have been. It is amazing to see how he's
adapted himself to the wild here yet remains as
completely attached to George as ever.*

It was excellent news that George had more
support and we planned to visit again later in the year.
But further letters informed us that life was quite
difficult for Christian and the other lions. Without Boy,
Christian on his own had not been able to defend the
territory around the camp, and a wild lion known as
'the Killer' had killed the engaging Supercub.

Christian had survived his fights with wild lions so
far, and George told us that his wounds were always on
his forelegs and shoulders, which demonstrated that he
had been fighting courageously.

*Christian had had a fight with a wild lion and
had two nasty gashes in his right foreleg. But he
did not seem the least perturbed about his
encounter and it was with much difficulty that I*

persuaded him to follow me back to camp, where I could attend to his injuries.

Christian was proving to be an exceptionally well adapted and brave young lion in this hostile environment, but growing frustrations became evident that could have had catastrophic consequences. One day he ambushed George and knocked him over, held him with his paws and took his head in his jaws. However, he released him quickly and George chased after him with a stick. Luckily George was not badly hurt, although a claw punctured his arm. Christian knew he had 'broken the rules', but soon after that he knocked Tony down, cuffed him with his paws and dragged him along by the head. Tony punched Christian hard on the nose and was immediately released, amazingly not badly injured either.

We were shocked when we heard about these incidents. Christian could easily have killed them, deliberately or not. George and Tony felt that the adolescent Christian was frustrated and lonely, and in a territory where he might never be able to live or establish a pride. The lionesses had mated with the wild lions, and while this was ideal for their rehabilitation it left Christian on his own. We sympathized with Christian's situation, and we appreciated more than ever how uniquely privileged we had been in our relationship with him. In the eight months with us in England, in very unnatural circumstances, he had never attacked anyone. Now that he was older and stronger, would our relationship with him change? How would he react with other visitors to Kora?

In August 1972, over a year after our reunion, we asked George if we could visit him and Christian, and meet Tony Fitzjohn. He responded enthusiastically, but warned us that he could not guarantee Christian would be around camp. The wild lions had driven him further up the Tana River, and he often spent weeks away. Nevertheless, we decided to go as there was always the possibility that George might be forced to leave Kora by changing circumstances, and there might not be another opportunity.

Tony met us in Nairobi and we could immediately see what an asset he must be at Kampi ya Simba and why George liked him so much. It is remarkable to think that today, so many years later, he is continuing George's conservation work at Mkomazi National Park in Tanzania, and is the Field Director of the George Adamson Wildlife Preservation Trust. In 2007 Tony was awarded an OBE for his services to conservation.

We arrived at the camp to find George suffering from flu but happy to see us, especially as we came with whisky and gin. He told us he had been hearing Christian mating with a wild lioness, so he was not far away, but it was not until the third night that to our great relief he appeared. Although he did not jump up on us like before, his greeting was as exuberant and as physical as ever. He was just as vocal, too, although his excited grunts were now much deeper. But he was enormous, and milling between us he knocked George over. George was not amused.

He believed that Christian was possibly the largest lion in Kenya, and certainly the largest lion in the immediate Tana area. He estimated his weight as close to five hundred pounds, though he was still only three years old and would continue to grow.

Over dinner we listened to George and Tony's stories of Christian's adventures, including his fights with the wild lions, and they gave us their accounts and interpretations of Christian's attacks on them both. It was clear that they both loved him and magnanimously did not bear any resentment over what they described as his adolescent frustration. We sat up talking all night with Christian interrupting us, entertaining us, and trying to push us off our chairs.

Ace wrote to his parents again.

We saw Christian every morning & evening for a walk and a chat. He is much calmer & much more self assured than last year, and stunning to be with. Just as silly. Huge. Jumped up on me only once as before on his hind legs and he did it extremely gently. He licked my face as he towered over me. He nearly crushed John by trying to sit on his lap!

Over the next few days we observed how much he had matured. While happy to greet us, he was even more independent than he had been the previous year. He dictated when he wanted to be with us and for how long, and he spent a lot of time outside the compound. Again we had absolutely no fear of him and looking back at the footage of the time we seem to be constantly patting and talking to him which he handled very patiently. He had now fully accepted Tony, and he was Tony's introduction to lions. Tony was to become an expert in bushcraft, and his diverse technical and mechanical skills were invaluable at Kampi ya Simba, greatly improving the camp's communications with the world.

This time we stayed nine days and saw more of the surrounding countryside. We went fishing with Terence, who often provided a welcome meal of fresh fish for us all. He was an expert on plant life, and pointed out among the thorn bushes and acacias the more exotic myrrh and frankincense shrubs. To us, the shapes of many of the plants and the washed-out colours looked different from equivalent semi-arid bush areas in Australia, but the two continents have a lot in common: a wide variety of climates and vegetations, open spaces, a far horizon, bright sunlight, clear blue skies, and an ancient peace and quiet. Interestingly, both George and Joy spoke to us about the possibility of breeding endangered African animals in remote wilderness areas of Australia and other countries, but nowadays it is clear that this on any scale would be a threat to already fragile ecological balances.

We read George's detailed reports to the Minister for Tourism and Wildlife, which were a fascinating and invaluable day by day record of a pride of lions over several years, particularly charting Christian's successful rehabilitation. In the past both George's and Joy's work had been criticized by some for not being 'scientific' enough, as they had not methodically recorded information to prescribed formulas. But after living with and observing particular animals over many years and several generations, by keeping diaries and notes, and by writing books and many letters, they have made a greater contribution than anyone else to our documented knowledge about lion behaviour.

Now that the lionesses had mated with the wild lions, Christian was rather isolated, and Tony was going to try to get a slightly younger male lion from the Nairobi Orphanage to be his companion. He may have been the nominal head of a pride, but the lionesses consorted with his enemy, and on his own he could not establish a territory here to raise his own cubs.

Christian was clearly ready to get on with a new stage of his life in the wild. Already he had spent extended periods away, possibly looking for a more suitable place to live. He had survived successfully so far, but we realized he might have to move far away, with the likelihood that none of us would ever see him again.

Back in Nairobi we staged a viewing of *The Lion at World's End* for various people who supported and appreciated the significance of George's work, including the Permanent Secretary, the Minister for Tourism and Wildlife and the Russian Ambassador to Kenya. Kampi ya Simba was an expensive camp to maintain, and there was no support from Joy, who was behaving predictably and blocking any funding for George's work from the Elsa Conservation Trust. Bill Travers had moved on to other projects and was currently working on a documentary with Jane Goodall about her work with chimpanzees. Income from Christian's documentaries helped fund George's work, and various visitors, supporters and admirers also contributed.

Back in London Tony Fitzjohn visited us with news that Christian was extremely well and a rather unusual peace treaty had been brokered between Christian and one of the wild lions. They were not friends, but roared to one another and left each other alone.

On the other hand, more worrying news was that some Somali tribesmen and their cattle had moved close to the camp. Christian had killed a few of their cattle and George was concerned he would be speared in retaliation. As it was illegal to have cattle in the area, the Game Department and the police moved the tribesmen on, but like the poachers who killed animals for ivory, body parts, hides and trophies, the Somali and their cattle would continue to create problems for George.

15

Christian's Pyramid

EARLY IN 1973 Christian crossed the Tana River, going north in the direction of the Meru National Park, a much more attractive area and a good hunting ground. In a National Park, animals were safer from poachers, hunters and tribesmen with cattle. Sadly, George finally stopped counting the days and months of Christian's absence from Kora and he was never seen again. For the next few years we waited for any news. We liked to imagine that he had established a territory and pride of his own a long way away, too far to return and visit George as he could not leave that pride unprotected. We hope that he lived another ten years, and that his descendants are hunting in Kenya today. He had miraculously returned to Africa, adapted quickly and survived the most dangerous years, and was big and strong. We could not regret anything.

During the first seven years at Kora, George

introduced seventeen lions. His rehabilitations were successful but the vicissitudes of life in the wild claimed many lives. Christian's rehabilitation was a complete success. In his autobiography *My Pride and Joy*, George refers to Christian's 'pyramid' rather than his 'pride'. He had heard Christian mating with wild lionesses on several occasions, so he could only assume that Christian had progeny and his own biological pride. However, Kampi ya Simba was made up of lions of various ages that George had selected from different sources, and through his knowledge and patience wove a coherent man-made 'pyramid' of lions around Christian. Juma and Lisa mated with a wild lion and had cubs, and some of them in turn had cubs. The pyramid complete, George did not want to import any more lions to the area, as that would create an imbalance of predators in a region where there was little game. He worked on his autobiography and continued documenting his observations of these next generations, including, we noted, that adolescent male lions at Kora were the most dangerous.

Kora was gazetted as a National Park in October

1973, which gave George and his lions government protection and official endorsement for his lion rehabilitation programme. George viewed Kora as a monument to 'the cheerful, mischievous, and courageous young lion from London'. He continued to live at Kora until 1989. One day a guest at the camp offered to go to the airstrip to meet more visitors. She was attacked on the road by poachers and George, who had heard the gunfire from the camp, was murdered by the poachers as he rushed to help her in his vehicle.

We feel honoured to have met George and are enormously grateful for his loving care of Christian. We witnessed the extraordinarily deep understanding and communication he had with his lions, and their love and trust in him, even allowing him to treat their injuries. Today he would be called a lion whisperer. His documented contribution to the world's knowledge about lions and conservation is immense, and like many others who were influenced by him we have supported wildlife and conservation causes ever since.

After *Born Free* there was an explosion of interest in Africa and wildlife, and Joy's publisher Sir William

Collins went on to publish many important books. These included Jane Goodall's *In the Shadow of Man* (1971), Mirella Ricciardi's photographic classic *Vanishing Africa* (1971), and various other books related to natural history and man's origins, such as Robert Ardrey's *The Territorial Imperative* (1966) and David Attenborough's *Life on Earth* (1979). People like these laid the foundation for today's conservation movements, and Joy was one of the first to articulate the significance of man's damaging and degrading relationship with the environment, as evidenced by the current forecasts about the effects of climate change.

A very sobering statistic is that the number of lions in Africa today has declined by two-thirds since Christian's time, making George's archive of information invaluable for the future. We are actively supporting related conservation projects, especially through the George Adamson Wildlife Preservation Trust.

John visited Kora by himself in 1973, and over the years has supported and visited other conservation projects in Kenya, Tanzania and South Africa. He is a

Trustee of the George Adamson Wildlife Preservation Trust (GAWPT) and he lectures on their behalf at the Royal Geographical Society and elsewhere. In addition, he works as a journalist and public relations consultant on travel and wildlife. In 2008 he was executive producer of *Mkomazi: The Return of the Rhino* about the relocation of four black rhinos from South Africa to Tony Fitzjohn at Mkomazi in Tanzania. John has been working with GAWPT on a proposal to revive the Kora National Park, which was virtually abandoned when George was murdered.

Ace returned to Australia, where he has a career as an art curator specializing in Australian Aboriginal and colonial art. In Africa we both bought textiles, carvings, beaded necklaces and artefacts for the first time, and we have both continued to collect tribal art since. Influenced by his visits to Africa, Ace wanted to know more about the original Aboriginal inhabitants of Australia. He discovered an extraordinarily diverse and rich artistic tradition and culture with an exciting contemporary expression, but also post-colonial dispossession, and much social and economic disadvantage.

With this YouTube-induced revival of interest in Christian, we have enjoyed reliving and reflecting on our time with him, looking at photographs, falling in love with him all over again, and missing him. Looking back, we cannot quite believe it turned out so well and we actually succeeded in returning Christian to Africa.

Christian had great charisma and it is what carried him through his life. He was chosen to be sent to Harrods for sale because he was attractive and had an even temperament. We found him irresistible, and against all reason bought him, while we were certainly not tempted by his sister Marta. When Bill Travers first contacted George in Kenya he described Christian as 'a very beautiful lion'. Christian starred in his own film. He became George's favourite and friend, and he was popular with people and lions. Kora was established because of Christian, and Christian's successful adaptation ensured that George remained there for nineteen years, and that Kora became a National Park.

Forty years later George's work is still continuing, and Christian's magic is again inspiring us to think about the interrelationship of all living creatures and the urgency for action on wildlife conservation. If everyone touched by Christian's story focused on addressing some of the key issues faced by the global community what could we achieve together in the spirit of his capacity for love and love of life?

The George Adamson Wildlife Preservation Trust

THE GEORGE ADAMSON WILDLIFE PRESERVATION TRUST was founded in 1980 by a group of George's friends and supporters. Following George's murder by poachers at Kora in 1989, Tony Fitzjohn, who had been George's assistant for eighteen years, became the Field Director of the Trust.

The original Chairman of the Trust was the late Dr Keith Eltringham, lecturer in Applied Biology at the University of Cambridge. The present Chairman is Bob Marshall Andrews QC, MP, and the Trustees are Alan Toulson and Andrew Mortimer (all old school friends of Tony's at Mill Hill School in London), Anthony Marrian, a Kenyan friend of George and Tony's, Major Bruce Kinloch MC, a former District Commissioner in Kenya and Chief Game Warden in Uganda, Tanzania and Malawi, and Brian Jackman the distinguished wildlife journalist and feature writer for the *Sunday*

Times. Additional UK Trustees are John Rendall, Paul Chauveau, James Lucas, Tim Peet and Peter Wakeham, all of whom bring relevant skills and experience to the development and well-being of the project. Trusts have also been established in the USA, Kenya, Tanzania, Germany and the Netherlands.

In 1989 the Royal Geographical Society hosted a reception for GAWPT to mark the launch of the Mkomazi Project in Tanzania.

The Mkomazi Game Reserve in northern Tanzania had become degraded, with rampant poaching, burning and hunting, and widespread human encroachment. In 1988 the Tanzanian government decided to restore the reserve as a wilderness area. Tony Fitzjohn, in conjunction with GAWPT, was offered the opportunity to work in partnership with the government on a multi-discipline programme of rehabilitation to embrace habitat restoration, infra-structural development, endangered species programmes for the African wild dog and the black rhino, community outreach programmes for the villages surrounding Mkomazi Game Reserve and an environmental education programme for school pupils from these villages.

Twenty years later Tony and the network of George Adamson trusts can proudly show that the financial support from generous friends and a number of notable charitable trusts has resulted in the upgrading of Mkomazi Game Reserve to National Park status, the establishment of a successful rhino sanctuary (the only one in Tanzania) and the implementation of an on-going captive breeding, veterinary and reintroduction programme for the African wild dog. Since George's death in 1989, Kora National Park has degenerated from lack of management, funding and protection from poaching and illegal grazing. The Trust is currently negotiating with the Kenyan Wildlife Services to return to Kora, restore George's camp and rehabilitate the Park.

George Adamson Wildlife Preservation Trust
16a Park View Road
London N3 2JB

THE WILDLIFE PRESERVATION TRUST

For additional information about GAWPT or to make a donation to continue the work of George Adamson please refer to the following websites:

In the UK: www.georgeadamson.org
In the USA: www.wildlifenow.com